Praise For

SUIT YOURSELF

"One of the biggest challenges investors face is between the ears. Learning how to manage our emotions and understanding why we do what we do goes a long way towards market success. Benjamin has written a book helping outline those challenges and how to overcome them by understanding our personality types. [As] someone who has experienced success in the markets, he gets why this will help us and has written it in a language we can all understand."

—Dave Ahern, cohost of the popular investing podcast *Investing for Beginners*

"Today, investing is more complicated than ever. So many variables are at play: risk, growth, value, duration, cyber vs real. It's intimidating. However, in *Suit Yourself*, Ben Tan has simplified the process by helping us understand our personal investment styles using an age-old approach (the Enneagram) and utilizing pop culture to make it fun and easily relatable. Bottom line: Investing comfort is based on more than just technical indicators. It's aligned with who we are and what we value. I highly recommend the book."

—Ed Zier, former chief operating officer of Baseline Financial Services

"The highest ROI activity you can do isn't analysis of a company or a sector; it's understanding yourself. Your personality offers insight into your own competitive advantages (and weaknesses!) as an investor. *Suit Yourself* helps you understand how you can leverage your own disposition to maximize your strengths and avoid your pitfalls. People are different. One person's gold mine is another person's land mine. Read this book to find out which is which for you."

—Nathan Worden, community manager, Yahoo Finance

"Benjamin Tan weaves his passion for the Enneagram, a framework that identifies and explains human motivations, with his deep knowledge of finance. This results in a practical guide specific to each Enneagram type to optimize their financial acumen and economic behaviors while leveraging the insights and strengths of their core types and overcoming their blind spots. Benjamin does a beautiful job in helping people recognize or validate their own Enneagram type (while learning all the others), with exemplars from popular movies and their characters, and provides not only clear development plans for each type's personal development but also type-specific customized pathways to financial success."

—Dr. R. Karl Hebenstreit, PhD, PCC, PHR, author, speaker, certified executive coach, consultant, Integrative 9 Enneagram Solutions faculty member, International Enneagram Association accredited professional with distinction

"Why do some people make risky investments and others stay in the safe harbor of savings accounts? *Suit Yourself* explores this idea through the lens of personality type, specifically one's Enneagram type. Uniquely blending psychology, finance, and pop culture, Benjamin Tan walks through the fiscal risks and rewards related to the style of each personality type. [Through the use of] fictional characters to embody these Enneagram types, the reader is shown road maps for investment strategies that align with their values. If you are looking to better understand the 'why' behind your personal investment strategy, you have just found your next great read."

—Tara Overzat, PhD, LPC, NCC, ACS, trauma therapist, educator, and advocate

"*Suit Yourself* is more than an investment guide—it goes beyond sound investment strategies and provides clarity into the emotional roller coaster of life. Why am I feeling this, and why do certain investments appeal to me more? Concise yet powerful, *Suit Yourself* provides an insightful path towards both financial investing as well as life itself. Definitely a book to have on any bookshelf, to read and to reflect upon repeatedly over time."

—Felicia Teng, certified public accountant, associate of the Society of Actuaries, founder of Get Counting

"Benjamin Tan offers a refreshingly intelligent and personalized road map to navigating the bewildering world of personal finance. By cleverly connecting personality psychology with investment strategy, he empowers readers to move beyond one-size-fits-all advice and build a financial future that's not just sound but authentically theirs."

—Joe Sipher, author of the award-winning *Outsmart the Learning Curve: How Ordinary People Can Achieve Extraordinary Success*

"Benjamin Tan's *Suit Yourself* provides an insightful exploration of investment strategies through the lens of the Enneagram personality framework. Through his entertaining use of pop culture references and personal stories, Tan turns complicated financial ideas into understandable concepts while providing customized investment strategies for people to match their portfolio choices with their personal characteristics. The book provides essential knowledge for individuals who want to manage their finances mindfully and with a clear goal."

—Dr. Patrick Behar-Courtois, author of *Maximizing Organizational Performance: A Guide to Effective Performance Coaching*

"In the digital age, connection is not just a luxury—it's a necessity. *Suit Yourself* brilliantly reminds us that authentic self-understanding and financial empowerment both begin with empathy and awareness. Benjamin's work reaffirms that even amid AI and algorithms, it's the human journey that drives true transformation."

—Dr. Brian Lambert, bestselling author of *The AI Lead*

SUIT YOURSELF:
A Portfolio Strategy for Every Personality Type
by Benjamin Tan

© Copyright 2025 Benjamin Tan

979-8-88824-754-9

All rights reserved. No part of this publication may be reproduced, stored in a retrieval system, or transmitted in any form or by any means—electronic, mechanical, photocopy, recording, or any other—except for brief quotations in printed reviews, without the prior written permission of the author.

Author photo credit: Matthew Kim
Designed by Suzanne Bradshaw

Published by

köehlerbooks™

3705 Shore Drive
Virginia Beach, VA 23455
800-435-4811
www.koehlerbooks.com

SUIT YOURSELF

A PORTFOLIO STRATEGY FOR EVERY PERSONALITY TYPE

BENJAMIN TAN

VIRGINIA BEACH
CAPE CHARLES

This book is dedicated to my husband, Blake, and our son, Paxton. You are the greatest investment I have ever made, with returns that enrich my life beyond measure. Your love inspires me to embrace profound changes and has shaped the person I am today. My heart is fuller because of you, and no other pursuit can compare.

Table of Contents

INTRODUCTION 1
    Folding Personality Typology
    into Personal Finance 4
    Hero's Journey in Pop Culture 5

CHAPTER 1
The Enneagram Model—A Map of Human Nature 7
    Making Sense of Complexities Through Clustering 8
    The Enneagram: A Guide to Human Nature 9
    Structural Explanation of the Enneagram Model 12
    Self-Understanding and
    Use of the Enneagram 19
    The Nine Enneagram Archetypes
    Illustrated Through Popular Culture 20
    Putting It Together: *Suit Yourself* 23

CHAPTER 2
Investment Road Map 25
    Asset Classes: More than Equities 26
    Everything Everywhere, but Not All at Once 36

CHAPTER 3
Type One:
Monica Geller (of *Friends*) 37
    Personality of Type Ones (Perfectionists) 39
    Checklist for Type One 41
    Type One Investors 42
    Type Ones: When Dealing with
    Investment Successes and Failures 47
    Road Map for Type One Investors 48
    Development Plan for Ones 52

CHAPTER 4
Type Two:
Katherine Johnson (of *Hidden Figures*) 55
    Personality of Type Twos (Givers) 57
    Checklist for Type Two 59
    Type Two Investors 60
    Type Twos: When Dealing with
    Investment Successes and Failures 64
    Road Map for Type Two Investors 65
    Development Plan for Twos 69

CHAPTER 5
Type Three:
Madonna 72
    Personality of Type Threes (Performers) 74
    Checklist for Type Three 76
    Type Three Investors 77
    Type Threes: When Dealing with
    Investment Successes and Failures 80
    Road Map for Type Three Investors 82
    Development Plan for Threes 85

CHAPTER 6
Type Four:
Cruella De Vil (of *Cruella*) 91
    Personality of Type Fours (Individualists) 93
    Checklist for Type Four 95
    Type Four Investors 96
    Type Fours: When Dealing with
    Investment Successes and Failures 100
    Road Map for Type Four Investors 101
    Development Plan for Fours 105

CHAPTER 7
Type Five:
Sherlock Holmes (of *Sherlock Holmes*) 108
- Personality of Type Fives (Investigators) 110
- Checklist for Type Five 111
- Type Five Investors 113
- Type Fives: When Dealing with
  Investment Successes and Failures 116
- Road Map for Type Five Investors 117
- Development Plan for Fives 121

CHAPTER 8
Type Six:
Maurizio Gucci (of *House of Gucci*) 124
- Personality of Type Sixes (Skeptics) 126
- Checklist for Type Six 128
- Type Six Investors 129
- Type Sixes: When Dealing with
  Investment Successes and Failures 133
- Road Map for Type Six Investors 134
- Development Plan for Sixes 137

CHAPTER 9
Type Seven:
Freddie Mercury (of *Bohemian Rhapsody*) 140
- Personality of Type Sevens (Enthusiasts) 142
- Checklist for Type Seven 143
- Type Seven Investors 144
- Type Sevens: When Dealing with
  Investment Successes and Failures 148
- Road Map for Type Seven Investors 149
- Development Plan for Sevens 153

CHAPTER 10
Type Eight:
Daenerys Targaryen (of *Game of Thrones*) 156
    Personality of Type Eights (Challengers) 158
    Checklist for Type Eight 160
    Type Eight Investors 161
    Type Eights: When Dealing with
    Investment Successes and Failures 165
    Road Map for Type Eight Investors 166
    Development Plan for Eights 169

CHAPTER 11
Type Nine:
Annie MacDuggan (of *The First Wives Club*) 173
    Personality of Type Nines (Peacemakers) 175
    Checklist for Type Nine 176
    Type Nine Investors 177
    Type Nines: When Dealing with
    Investment Successes and Failures 181
    Road Map for Type Nine Investors 182
    Development Plan for Nines 186

CHAPTER 12
My Ongoing Enneagram and Financial Journey 191
    Biggest Investing Mistakes
    Made and Lessons Learned 203
    Staying Present with
    an Abundant Mindset 208

EPILOGUE 211
    Closing Thoughts 214

ACKNOWLEDGMENTS 217

REFERENCES 219

INTRODUCTION

Even as I pursued a well-compensated career in banking and attained early financial independence, I struggled to find my way in the world. Raised without a mother in public housing, I kept to myself amid the motley crew of relatives who took turns providing the necessities. I wouldn't live with my father until I turned thirteen. He lived alone for most of my childhood, focusing on working multiple jobs and finishing his diploma. As a result, my emotional needs went unnoticed, and I learned to disconnect from them over time. Growing up gay in Singapore, a country that outlawed homosexuality until recently, was an added challenge. I found it hard to make genuine connections with people for fear of rejection.

To survive, I strove to be as self-sufficient as possible, relying on no one—not even an employer for a paycheck. My early financial goals were driven by an unconscious desire to isolate myself because I did not wish to risk getting hurt by people again. Yet the more autonomy I earned, the more confused I became. And the void in my inner world did not go away. So I became fascinated with psychology and self-help books as a way to reconcile my past.

Since arriving in America in 2021, not only have I had a chance to engage in more profound inner work to unravel my family origins, but I also took the opportunity to commence a graduate program in clinical mental health counseling and cocreated a mental health technology start-up, Psyntel, with my friend and cofounder, Sam Fargo. Part of that self-discovery process also led me to the Enneagram, a personality typology that has helped me to both accept myself and imagine new possibilities.

Research on the Enneagram personality types showed me how many of my past financial and nonfinancial decisions had been driven by unconscious biases, blind spots, fixations, and a scarcity mindset. I was oblivious to my longing for connection with the world, trust in others, and, most importantly, love. Only in recent years have I realized the vital interconnections among the mind, heart, and body.

The Enneagram also paved the way for a fresh perspective on investing—specifically, of how we must become more aware of our mental, emotional, and visceral faculties beneath the superficial notions of who we believe we are. Otherwise, we risk getting hijacked by our shadow selves (these unconscious aspects of ourselves) and making financial decisions based on childhood coping mechanisms rather than rationality. To become better investors, our portfolio strategies must resonate with our innate selves. A one-size-fits-all methodology is neither compatible nor sustainable.

Matching portfolio strategies to personality types thus became a primary thesis I pursued with equal parts curiosity and passion. I felt it was my calling to marry my expertise in finance, experience with personal investing, insights into clinical psychology, and a lifelong passion for pop culture into an accessible but powerful system to help readers on their road to financial empowerment. At the same time, I wanted to develop a message with an empathetic voice that would honor individuality.

That is the origin story of *Suit Yourself*.

VOLATILITY IN THE WORLD OF FINANCE

With round-the-clock news coverage and media outlets fighting for clicks, every headline has the potential to trigger a price move. A tweet from Elon Musk can send the markets up or down in seconds. Anyone with a smartphone can place instant bets on the price direction of nearly any asset—from commodities to cryptocurrencies—through gamified trading and gambling apps. Add algorithmic high-frequency trading to the equation, and you could argue that we are now living inside the world's largest casino.

If that sounds like hyperbole, consider GameStop's meteoric rise and fall in 2021. Hyped by the Reddit group Wall Street Bets, the stock went up even as the company's fundamentals suffered, triggering a short squeeze that sent prices even higher. At one point, GameStop hit $483. Then, it crashed to below $20. While the popular trading platform Robinhood has democratized investing, it has also gamified it, fueling sentiment-driven meme stocks and incentivizing inexperienced investors to make risky bets.

The GameStop fiasco made for an entertaining story, but the issue is serious, and the stakes are high. Young adults in America are experiencing alarming rates of financial distress, and for obvious reasons. They are contending with an ongoing generational wealth gap, crushing student debt, and other economic uncertainties like inflation. They know they need to take control of their financial destinies. To some extent, the influx of new investors is a positive development, but to be unconscious and undisciplined in one's approach to investing (as demonstrated by the meme stock phenomenon) can do more harm than good.

TEMPTATION TO COPY

Too much financial advice falls into a simplistic one-size-fits-all prescription. There are over 2,000 books analyzing Warren Buffett alone. Most financial self-help literature is prescriptive, based on specific asset classes and processes that worked for the authors. Readers are encouraged to follow the methodologies without first considering suitability. Most people, however, do not share the personality types of said writers. Trying to imitate their strategies when one's disposition may be the exact opposite is likely to result in more stress and losses than rewards. Yet the temptation to copy them is strong. Replication, after all, is part of our DNA.

Strategies of the world's greatest investors rarely fall neatly into one category. Some make their wealth primarily from real estate, while others may have an unbelievable eye for collectibles. Warren Buffett is often cited for championing index funds. Yet he built his wealth with savvy, high-conviction, high-concentration stock positions because he is an exceptional (and cerebral) individual with a unique character.

Each path to success is different; everything depends on the individual on that journey. By the same token, our approach to investing must be our own, tailored according to individual temperament. The path should resonate with our innate selves but also be capable of adapting with time as we evolve. In addition, we should not limit ourselves to the stock market. Real estate, fixed income, savings, and other assets are just as applicable in portfolio construction. Depending on the traits of a given personality type, some asset classes might be more suitable than others, while others should be avoided.

FOLDING PERSONALITY TYPOLOGY INTO PERSONAL FINANCE

Suit Yourself incorporates personality typing into the finance genre. Using principles from said typology, this book guides readers to understand their unconscious tendencies and how mental, emotional, and instinctual leanings can play out in investment decisions.

Compared to other personality theories, such as the Myers-Briggs Type Indicator, Enneagram teachings are more fluid and nuanced. No one is put in a box, because our thinking, feeling, and instinctive patterns are not hardwired. While they result from childhood coping mechanisms and lived experiences, we continue to evolve and can make shifts. This psychological model identifies unique dispositions across nine archetypes and maps out pathways for individuals to adopt counterbalancing characteristics of other archetypes as they mature in self-awareness. Like the yin-yang philosophy of Taoism, the Enneagram sees human nature as a constant evolution with, more significantly, infinite potential to grow. This more mutable perspective on individual temperament and investing is central to this book.

In the end, readers do not have to subscribe to the Enneagram theory to glean useful advice from this book any more than they must believe in Taoism to enjoy the wisdom of books like *The Tao of Physics*. I am simply offering a fresh lens through which to see a familiar subject. *The Tao of Physics* reached many readers who might have previously found physics dry and unrelatable. Similarly, many young adults find that books about investing are overly technical and do not speak to the realities of their lives. Here I use the Enneagram (and a dose of pop culture humor) to help readers discover their personality types and the unique traits associated with each before finding an investing style that suits them.

I do not stipulate a specific journey to take, but I do illustrate the hidden motivations, fears, blind spots, and potential pitfalls of each investor type. Different road maps are laid out, correlating portfolio mix and possible action plans with specific strengths, weaknesses, and developmental directions of the nine personality types.

HERO'S JOURNEY IN POP CULTURE

My decision to illustrate the nine archetypes through iconic film and television characters serves an essential purpose: to see our lives as a hero's journey. The most significant life changes happen when we find ourselves (reluctantly) in new situations where we must snap out of homeostasis. As investors, we may view our paths to financial freedom as a learning, growth, and self-discovery journey. Volatility in the financial markets, black swan events like COVID-19, and all other vicissitudes of life are the proverbial dragons we must slay to achieve confidence as investors and clarify our identities.

Movies and television have long provided vivid illustrations of a hero's journey. Consider Dorothy in *The Wizard of Oz* (1939). Her companions on the Yellow Brick Road (the Scarecrow, the Tin Man, and the Cowardly Lion) are personifications of the qualities (intellect, heart, and courage) she must acquire for her journey home.

Using a more modern Marvel reference, think of all the origin stories, like Iron Man, Spider-Man, and Doctor Strange. These are characters forced to confront difficult circumstances before surpassing their original makeup to become something bigger.

We often turn to pop culture to make sense of our own stories and seek reassurance. Reflecting on my early fondness for movies and television shows, in rooting for the underdogs I was perhaps rooting for myself to overcome my challenges. I was also (and still am) drawn to strong female characters, mostly likely due to an intense yearning for the protection of a maternal figure.

This is why *Suit Yourself* taps into the power of storytelling and pop culture to give life to each of the nine basic personality archetypes. The result is a one-of-a-kind financial self-help creation that I hope will speak to readers. My wish is for this book to inspire, entertain, and inform, helping others discover themselves as investors, and maybe as people too.

Chapter 1

The Enneagram Model— A Map of Human Nature

> "This map is going to be your guide to North Shore. . . . You got your freshmen, ROTC guys, preps, JV jocks, Asian nerds, cool Asians, varsity jocks, unfriendly Black hotties, girls who eat their feelings, girls who don't eat anything, desperate wannabes, burnouts, sexually active band geeks, the greatest people you will ever meet . . . and the worst. Beware of Plastics."
>
> *Mean Girls (2004)*

The movie *Mean Girls* is a sharp-witted commentary on cliques in high schools. Impressively, Tina Fey adapted the script from a self-help book—*Queen Bees and Wannabes: Helping Your Daughter Survive Cliques, Gossip, Boyfriends, and the New Realities of Girl World*—and not a novel.

In an early scene, new student Cady Heron (played by Lindsay Lohan) is introduced to her peers at North Shore High School by Janice Ian via a hand-drawn map. Back then, things were not so digital. That map divides the students into a collection of over-the-top and oh-so politically incorrect stereotypes. Janice Ian would get canceled today if that map had gone viral. Nevertheless, in the movie, categorizing the North Shore folks into various tribes does help Heron make sense of her peers. Heron starts observing her social boundaries—as defined on the map—and finds her rhythm, befriending only Ian and Damian Leigh.

Dramedy ensues, however, when she crosses into other territories, joining both the Plastics (the worst people at North Shore, according to Ian) and Mathletes (social suicide) against the expressed wishes of her clique. That very crossing forms the catalyst for Heron's character development.

There would be no movie if she had merely stayed in her own lane.

MAKING SENSE OF COMPLEXITIES THROUGH CLUSTERING

We are often told that stereotyping is wrong. Humans are unique, and we need to honor individuality. But our world is organized (and recorded) based on categories: nationalities, ethnicities, educational qualifications, professions, political affiliations, religions, and so on. When joining any new establishment or club or seeking new opportunities, whether professional, financial, political, or social, individuals often provide a litany of information that helps administrators (or, more likely these days, algorithms) infer everything from job suitability and romantic matches to creditworthiness and likelihood of terrorism, based on historical patterns.

Grouping helps humans make sense of the world by simplifying and systematizing information to better fit the rational part of our brains. Organization by clusters helps us recall, identify, predict, and respond, giving us greater clarity. With it, we can better handle randomness and a jumble of information.

THE ENNEAGRAM: A GUIDE TO HUMAN NATURE

What if we were given a guide to understanding human nature equivalent to the map of North Shore High School's cafeteria in *Mean Girls*? Imagine possessing an intuitive conceptual framework that helps us understand and respond better to the complexities of people—a map that goes beyond observable human behaviors by providing rich insights into underlying motivations organized by personality types.

Enter the Enneagram.

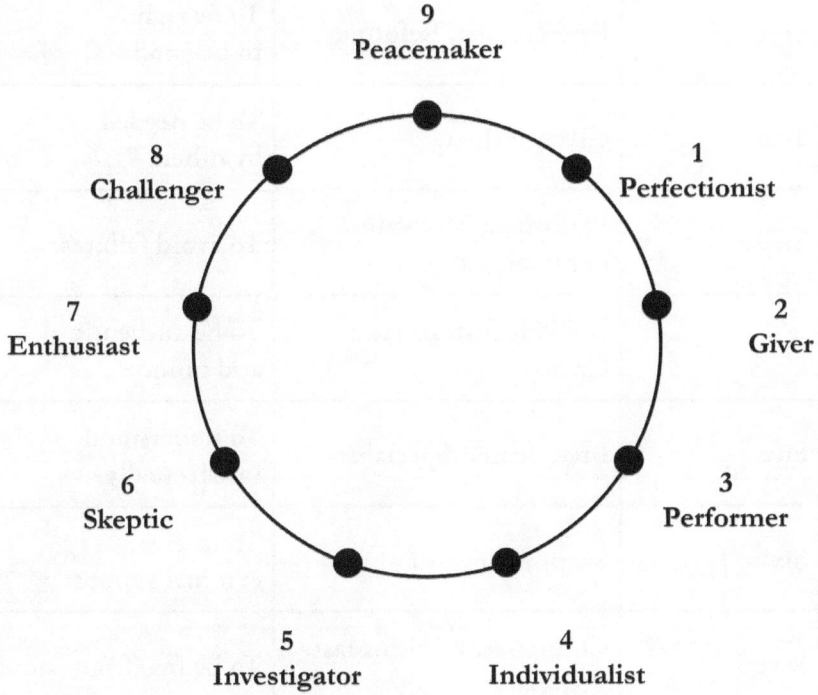

The Enneagram is a model of nine interconnected archetypal personalities, as represented by nine equidistant points on the circumference of a circle. Instead of "desperate wannabes" and "sexually active band geeks," we now have Enneagram types identified by neutral numerals, from Type One to Type Nine. Moreover, this diagram does not single out anyone as purely negative, like the Plastics.

Below are the common names and primary motivations associated with each Enneagram type:

Enneagram Type	Commonly Known As...	Primary Motivation(s)
One	Perfectionist, Reformer	To be right, to be good
Two	Giver, Helper	To be needed by others
Three	Performer, Motivator, Achiever	To avoid failures
Four	Individualist, Intense Creative	To be authentic and unique
Five	Investigator, Specialist	To understand intellectually
Six	Skeptic, Loyalist	To receive external support
Seven	Connoisseur, Enthusiast, Visionary	To be free from pain

Eight	Challenger, Leader	To have control and power
Nine	Peacekeeper, Peacemaker	To create peace and harmony

Enneagram-esque teachings have been explored through different lenses and evolved contextually over centuries. It has been suggested that Odysseus encounters each of the nine personality types in Homer's *Odyssey*, written in the eighth century BCE. In modern times, the Enneagram has found applications in personal growth, leadership training, and therapy-informed executive coaching.

The basic Enneagram principle is that everyone can best identify with a single personality archetype (out of the nine). While we may recognize behavioral traits of multiple Enneagram types, we each possess one core operating system (in software speak), located in the inner recesses of the psyche. Multiple individuals can exhibit similar behaviors, but if their underlying reasons for said behaviors are poles apart, they do not possess the same personalities. For example, extroverted corporate climbers are likely Type Ones (perfectionists) if their primary instinct is to reform organizational policies and make things right based on their high-minded ideals. A similar-looking mover and shaker may be closer to a Type Three (performer) if all that effort is based on an emotional need for professional and personal recognition. In other words, underlying motivations, fixations, and latent underpinnings constitute the personality inference process, not actions.

Childhood, inborn disposition, and prenatal factors contribute to forming our basic personalities, which begin taking shape by the time we develop a consciousness separate from our caretakers. Our interactions with and orientations toward the adults who raised us are foundational to building identity. From there, coping strategies, adaptive responses, worldviews, defenses, and other features of our inner landscapes grow in complexity and depth. One's core Enneagram type does not change over a lifetime, just as a Windows laptop does not turn into a MacBook; but the operating system does get upgraded—if one elects to reboot—over time to become more sophisticated and powerful.

The Enneagram system offers one of the best psychological frameworks for introspection because it looks beneath the surface of human manners to explore the underbelly. Dividing personalities into distinct archetypes also allows for easier recognition of self and others. The theory has become popular in recent years, enjoying increasing scientific validation and expanding use cases. Major corporations such as Boeing, Google, and Microsoft have used the Enneagram in their employee training to increase productivity and foster teamwork.

STRUCTURAL EXPLANATION OF THE ENNEAGRAM MODEL

Points on the Enneagram circle are connected via lines. Each type is connected to two more, which correlate to the behavioral shifts (good and bad) people make during stress and security. Type One (perfectionist), for example, is linked to Types Four (individualist) and Seven (enthusiast). Because it is a circle, every type also has two adjacencies known as wings, which provide further contextual gradients to the typology. Referring again to Type One (perfectionist), the wings are Types Nine (peacemaker) and Two (giver).

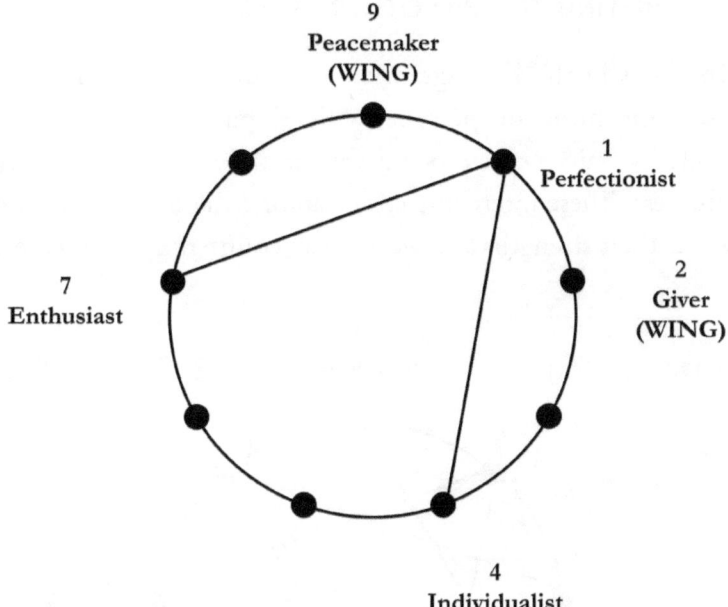

MOVEMENT IN THE ENNEAGRAM CIRCLE

There would be no dramedy or *Mean Girls* if Cady Heron had remained friends with her squad of the "greatest people"—Janice Ian and Damian Leigh—at North Shore. In Enneagram theory, we grow when we learn from other personality types through lines and wings. Because Heron makes those daring social leaps at North Shore, she learns how to wear pink on Wednesdays, understands that ruining Regina George's life does not make her any happier, and deduces that the limit does not exist for that sudden-death question to win the Mathlete state championship.

For meaningful personal development, we must make an intentional effort to move beyond our core archetypes and adopt the winning traits of others. We should aspire to assume qualities from types interconnected in the Enneagram—especially lines—to compensate for inherent shortcomings and augment our strong suits.

LINES: PIVOTING TO TWO OTHER TYPES

The lines in the Enneagram circle connect every point to two others, representing key personality development directions as well as unhealthy traits a core type inhabits in times of stress and lack of mindfulness. These interconnections among the three points are by design, as their strengths and weaknesses counterbalance each other.

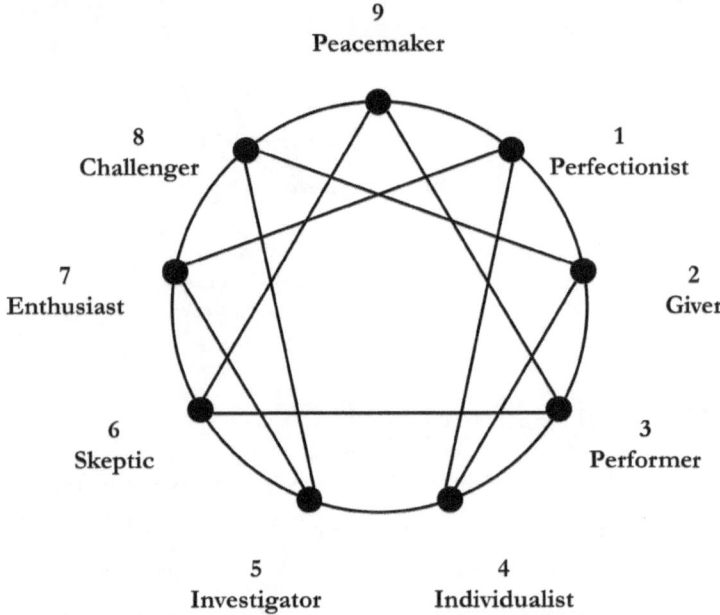

These lines are referred to by various names. Some writers use the terms "integration" and "disintegration," with the former representing growth and the latter signaling a decline. However, I prefer to view both as pivots, free from rigid ranking. In reality, people are just as capable of embodying the strengths of their disintegration points when they move toward greater self-awareness as they are of succumbing to the reactive behaviors of their integration points when triggered. Our level of consciousness—how present and self-aware we are—determines whether these points become sources of personal elevation or stumbling blocks.

Enneagram Type	Weakness	Pivots and Their Counterbalancing Qualities
One (Perfectionist)	Rigidity	Four (Self-Reflection) Seven (Spontaneity)
Two (Giver)	Self-Denial	Four (Introspection) Eight (Self-Advocacy)
Three (Performer)	Vanity	Six (Esprit de Corps) Nine (Harmony)
Four (Individualist)	Envy	One (Steadfastness) Two (Empathy)
Five (Investigator)	Insulation	Seven (Experientialism) Eight (Assertiveness)
Six (Skeptic)	Self-Doubt	Three (Self-Direction) Nine (Trust)
Seven (Enthusiast)	Escape	One (Discipline) Five (Contemplation)
Eight (Challenger)	Control	Two (Selflessness) Five (Observation)
Nine (Peacemaker)	Repression	Three (Self-Agency) Six (Discernment)

For example, Type Seven personalities embody enthusiasm and love of external experiences. When they are healthy—mindful and conscious in actions—this archetype tempers their passion for more with self-restraint and integrity, both key strengths of Type Ones (perfectionists). Instead of throwing caution to the wind, they slow down to practice quiet contemplation and conserve resources, like measured Type Fives (investigators). On the other hand, unhealthy Type Seven enthusiasts who are ego-driven, especially in times of stress, can become harsh and critical, overstepping boundaries like pompous police officers, recalling angry Type One perfectionists. In investing, this uncompromising thinking may lead to doubling down or giving up when it is not in their best interest. They may also ride on their intellectual high horses and alienate others, echoing how insular Type Five investigators may act in distress. This might manifest as being less receptive to external advice or alternative perspectives when deciding how to invest.

Being cognizant of our potential shadow traits allows us to catch ourselves before doing anything rash. Whether we achieve positive development toward a healthier self or decline into our unhealthy egos, bearing two pivots in mind offers richer insights and renewed references to improve past performances. Cady Heron of *Mean Girls* would not have become Spring Fling queen and learned her life lessons had she not joined both Plastics and Mathletes.

WINGS: MOVING IN ADJACENCIES

Our personalities exist on a continuum—the Enneagram model is a circle, after all—and we have characteristics that extend beyond our primary types. "Wings" references the two Enneagram types on the left and right of each point in the diagram, providing further nuance to the typology. One wing is usually more dominant than the other. As a Type Five investigator, my wings are Types Four (individualism) and Six (skepticism), but the former (part of the "heart" triad, which I address below) is more pronounced in my personality than the latter (part of the "head" triad). As an investor, I am inclined to be emotional versus skeptical in my decision-making.

Paying attention to our wings raises our self-awareness, helping us understand and respond better to the external environment.

THE HEAD, HEART, AND GUT

The Enneagram is also divided into three triads, broadly describing how we process and respond to information.

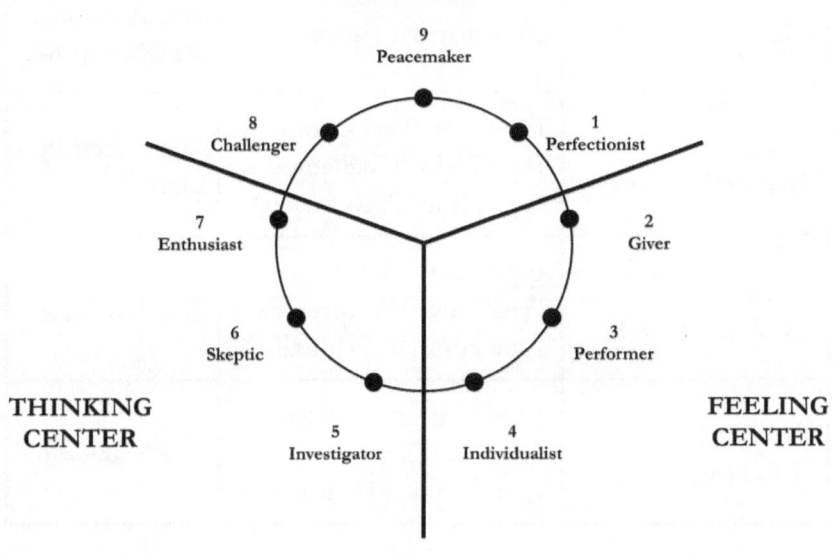

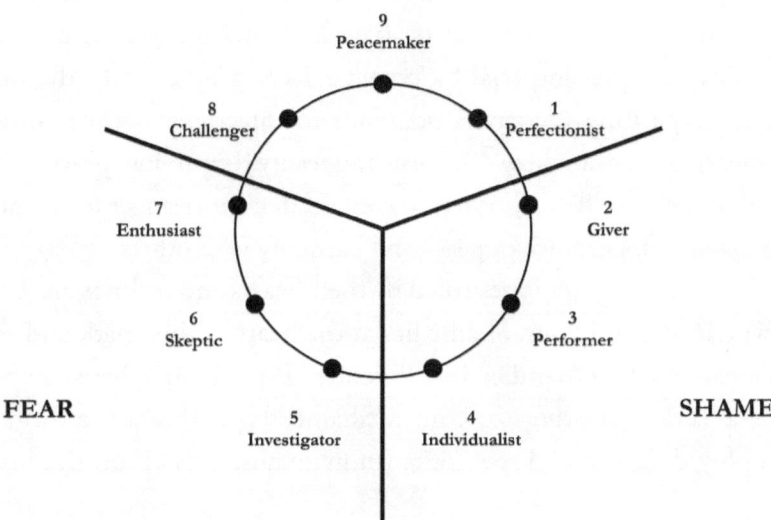

Let's return to the 1939 classic film *The Wizard of Oz*. The Cowardly Lion craves courage, the Tin Man desires a heart, and the Scarecrow wants a brain. The three characters yearn for what they lack the most, and their aspirations match the three Enneagram triads.

Triad	Enneagram Types	The Wizard of Oz Character
Gut (Instinctive Center)	Type One (Perfectionist) Type Eight (Challenger) Type Nine (Peacemaker)	The Cowardly Lion
Heart (Feeling Center)	Type Two (Giver) Type Three (Performer) Type Four (Individualist)	The Tin Man
Head (Thinking Center)	Type Five (Investigator) Type Six (Skeptic) Type Seven (Enthusiast)	The Scarecrow

The gut triad is ruled by anger, which can manifest itself outwardly, inwardly, or a mix of the two. Type Eight (challenger) is the most dominant, expressing rage by commandeering others. On the other hand, Type One (perfectionist) tends to direct that feeling inward, fomenting a tension between ideals and reality. Type Nine (peacemaker) is ultimately conflicted, trying to contain that inner anger to maintain an external appearance of peace and harmony with others.

The Enneagram types ruled by their hearts and feelings are Types Two, Three, and Four. Shame lies at the heart of this triad, and each Enneagram type handles it differently. Type Twos (givers) rely on the affection of others to control shame, Type Threes (performers) employ denial, and Type Fours (individualists) dwell on the inside of their emotional landscapes.

Intellect is the driving force behind Types Five, Six, and Seven. These Enneagram archetypes cope with fears using their heads as they react to situations and relationships. Type Fives (investigators) tend to withdraw into their minds, Type Sixes (skeptics) seek confirmation from external sources to allay their inner doubts, and Type Sevens (enthusiasts) embrace outside stimuli to escape.

SELF-UNDERSTANDING AND USE OF THE ENNEAGRAM

In theory, we should all know ourselves better than we know anything else since we inhabit our bodies, hearts, and minds around the clock. In practice, self-understanding is more complicated. We are inclined to acknowledge our positive attributes—generous, easygoing, all-around amazeballs—but become uncomfortable when certain unattractive qualities emerge. Often, we fall back on fundamental attribution bias: We excuse our less-than-desirable qualities by attributing them to external factors, whereas for others, we make character judgments. Consider the following scenario: "I was late to the meeting because traffic was bad" versus "Peter was late; he is so irresponsible."

It is precisely those inconvenient (and sometimes ugly) truths that we need to unpack in search of self-awareness. No one is perfect, and we always have room for improvement. Acknowledging our limitations, narrow paradigms, insecurities, unhealthy fixations, blind spots, and defensiveness is the first step toward creating a better version of ourselves. This is where the Enneagram is most valuable—as an unbiased tool for self-appraisal.

When dealing with money, it is easy for deeply wired triggers and ingrained fears to take over reactions. We can indeed be our own worst enemies. Self-understanding is hence crucial to our lifelong investing journeys. To reach our financial goals, or any goal, we must dig into our counterproductive personality traits and learn to handle them with clarity and consistency.

THE NINE ENNEAGRAM ARCHETYPES ILLUSTRATED THROUGH POPULAR CULTURE

Below is an overview of the nine archetypes, using popular fictional and nonfictional film or television characters (and one very famous personality), as a prelude to the upcoming chapters, where their investing behaviors are further deciphered.

TYPE ONE (PERFECTIONIST): MONICA GELLER (OF *FRIENDS*)

Before Marie Kondo normalized neatness, the fictional Monica Geller was the poster child for perfectionists everywhere. Type Ones care about details, and their approach to investing is meticulous, reliable, and methodical. On the other hand, their fondness for order and predictability can make it challenging to handle the inevitable uncertainty of investing.

TYPE TWO (GIVER): KATHERINE JOHNSON (OF *HIDDEN FIGURES*)

Hidden Figures (2016) is a biographical film about female African American mathematicians who worked at the National Aeronautics and Space Administration (NASA) in the 1960s. The main character, Katherine Johnson, embodies the helpful and self-sacrificial facets of a Type Two. While Type Two investors are humble and less prone to unchecked greed when managing money, they may struggle with financial self-enrichment out of guilt. Yet, as with all charitable people, growing or protecting resources is as necessary as giving them away. Therefore, Type Twos must establish their investment goals within a profoundly personalized and purpose-driven framework.

TYPE THREE (PERFORMER): MADONNA

Madonna typifies the Type Three personality: goal-oriented, competitive, and always in vogue. As laser-focused as they are, Type Threes tend to avoid the possibility of failure and can be very image-conscious. Investing to win is a different mindset from investing in order to not lose. A general fear of missing out may compel a Type Three investor to jump onto investment bandwagons to maintain an image of being part of the zeitgeist.

TYPE FOUR (INDIVIDUALIST): CRUELLA DE VIL (OF *CRUELLA*)

Type Fours enjoy wearing their personalities on their sleeves. Cruella De Vil (the Emma Stone version) is the perfect Type Four embodiment: brilliant, alluring, and complex. Her transformation on-screen from homeless shoplifter to fashion powerhouse is one for the ages. Taken too far, however, she may morph into the Glenn Close version: self-absorbed and destructive. Type Four investors tend to be creative in their financial pursuits, but guardrails are essential to minimize an "I feel, therefore I am" style of decision-making, which can lead to arbitrary and capricious capital deployments.

TYPE FIVE (INVESTIGATOR): SHERLOCK HOLMES (OF *SHERLOCK HOLMES*)

It is no coincidence that Type Fives are commonly known as investigators. The 2009 movie *Sherlock Holmes* captures that archetypal blend of eccentricity and intelligence mixed with social awkwardness and loneliness. As investors, Type Fives are suited to doing due diligence to size up opportunities. On the other hand, they are equally prone to getting stuck in their mental loops and holding back from investing altogether.

TYPE SIX (SKEPTIC): MAURIZIO GUCCI (OF *HOUSE OF GUCCI*)

What would Maurizio Gucci have accomplished if Patrizia Reggiani had not had him killed? In the film *House of Gucci* (2021), he undergoes a full Type Six makeover, from anxious law student to formidable usurper of his uncle's stake in Gucci. A Type Six investor tends to be in a constant state of polarity, shuffling back and forth between bull and bear cases. Anxiety management is vital to sustainable and confident investing (especially early in the journey).

TYPE SEVEN (ENTHUSIAST): FREDDIE MERCURY (OF *BOHEMIAN RHAPSODY*)

Freddie Mercury was known for his larger-than-life persona. His song "I Want It All" sums up the essence of Type Seven (enthusiast) personalities. Restraint is critical to securing their financial future—and survival, for that matter. They must reconcile investing (a form of delayed gratification) with their insatiable and impulsive nature.

TYPE EIGHT (CHALLENGER): DAENERYS TARGARYEN (OF *GAME OF THRONES*)

For eight seasons, the world watched Daenerys Targaryen and her blond ambition inch closer to the Iron Throne, only for her to be stabbed to death by her nephew-lover Jon Snow in the last episode. Type Eights (challengers) crave power, and money is power to them. Come hell or high water, they will raise the necessary capital to become apex predators. However, if unchecked, their lust can backfire and lead to impulsive investments.

TYPE NINE (PEACEMAKER):
ANNIE MACDUGGAN (OF *THE FIRST WIVES CLUB*)

Of the three first wives in the 1996 film, Annie MacDuggan has the most dramatic story arc, transforming herself from a neurotic ex-wife who still pines for reconciliation to an equity partner at her ex-husband's advertising agency. She is a Type Nine (peacemaker) upgraded to her best self, partly by unleashing her inner warrior. As investors, Type Nines may feel minimal action is the best way to maintain their inner peace. These peacemakers can become more effective investors if they pick the proper asset allocations, inner circles, and approaches to pursuing their agenda.

PUTTING IT TOGETHER:
SUIT YOURSELF

To me, psychological and financial self-help genres are intimately connected; a firm self-understanding must work in lockstep with a successful financial journey.

In this book, we will use the Enneagram to heighten our self-awareness and increase our effectiveness regarding financial decisions. This will help readers develop personalized investing road maps that resonate with their core personality types. To copy what others are investing (or to merely adopt a risk-adjusted portfolio model from financial advisers) without first realizing one's hidden fears, biases, blind spots, triggers, vulnerabilities, and fixations surrounding the highly charged topic of money is neither sustainable nor reassuring. Realizing who we are, why we do the things we do, and how we do them allows us to create a more straightforward road to our financial goals—with less cognitive dissonance from trying to fit a square peg into a round hole.

To reiterate, no one fits perfectly into a single Enneagram type, and no one theory can fully describe all shades of personality. Even the combination of lines and wings providing additional dimensions to each core archetype will not explain everything about us. One should think of the Enneagram as a cognitive tool—and not a pigeonhole—to uncover one's deeper self over a lifetime. Another central objective of this book is to maintain that no Enneagram type is superior to another, which applies equally to approaches to personal investing. All archetypes can be successful. The key is to play to the strengths of each personality and establish appropriate guardrails to minimize pitfalls.

Readers will be guided to use the Enneagram to identify their core archetypes before exploring specific investment road maps tailored to their personalities. One should also examine the profiles of related pivots and wings to gain a fuller picture of oneself and others.

When the investing road gets tough or heady, and it always does, we become even more susceptible to the blind spots and fixations of our own archetypes and those of our pivots and wings. We must raise our self-awareness on this long, winding road to keep moving forward.

Chapter 2

Investment Road Map

Few fund managers drew more ire and controversy than Catherine Wood of Ark Invest in the twenty-first century. She is arguably the first female icon in the industry to have reached the same prominence as Warren Buffett and Peter Lynch. Famed for her bullish take on the future of disruptive technologies, she made a significant bet on Tesla in the late 2010s, well before Model 3 was successfully mass-produced and back when the electric carmaker (along with founder Elon Musk) was dealing with bad publicity. Like George Soros, who made a fortune and a name for himself when he wagered big against the Great British pound in 1992, Wood ascended to the pantheon of greats when her $4,000 Tesla stock price prediction—widely mocked by Wall Street and the press—came true in early 2021.

Since then, Wood has become synonymous with bold predictions and even bolder bets. She envisages a different world to come, one dominated by cutting-edge modernizations, ranging from autonomous ridesharing and gene editing to 3D printing and space exploration. You will not hear her preach about Costco or, God forbid, Saudi Aramco. Wood and Ark Invest foresee grocery deliveries via drones and a future powered by renewable energy.

When markets rotated out of growth stocks starting in late 2021, all the funds managed by Ark Invest tanked by more than 50 percent over the course of 2022. In comparison, the S&P 500 fell by less than 20 percent. Ark Invest funds underperformed because almost all the underlying assets shared close-knit price correlations: They were growth-oriented, loss-making, and heavily dependent on easy access to low-cost capital. As a result of such skewed allocations, many commentators accused Wood of mismanagement and irresponsibility.

Only time can judge Ark Invest and Catherine Wood. Apple and Microsoft took decades to find their footing before becoming multitrillion-dollar companies, so it remains to be seen how Ark Invest and its stock picks will fare.

ASSET CLASSES: MORE THAN EQUITIES

Only some people can stomach price swings like Wood—or collect a fixed percentage of management fee based on assets under management. Most investors cannot handle such a significant drop in value; the psychological stress and risk of emotional capitulation at the worst times can exact a steep cost in personal and financial well-being.

The lesson we can now learn from Catherine Wood is that overall portfolio composition must not just comprise growth stocks. Concentration risks can be fatal. There is more to equity investing than emerging technology names and more to investing than the stock market alone. For individual wealth to be more resilient in the worst of times, one needs to diversify into different asset classes. Portfolio allocations should provide meaningful counterbalances in price movements to minimize large negative swings.

It must be noted that healthy cash reserves are essential at any stage of the investment journey in case of unexpected life events. Repayment of expensive personal borrowings—including student loans and credit card debt—should also precede investing. Being leveraged with low cash reserves and having to sell portfolio assets for liquidity during the worst market conditions is a situation to avoid.

The four broad investment classes to be discussed are as follows:

» Real estate

» Stocks

» Fixed income

» Alternative investments (yes, Bitcoin is included here)

When outlining investment road maps for the nine Enneagram types in this book, references are made to some or all the above asset classes based on their relevance to unique personality traits. It is therefore essential to frame each asset class and its subcategories before delving into the Enneagram chapters.

Diversification will not eliminate risks altogether. Increased globalization and the instant flow of information have caused prices of more asset classes to move in tandem over the short term, albeit not with the kind of amplification one would experience if invested in a single asset class—or, worse, if they went all-in on cryptocurrency after actor Matt Damon said, "Fortune favors the brave" in a Crypto.com commercial that aired during the Super Bowl in 2022. Was Damon brave enough to be paid in digital currencies, or did he take good old-fashioned cash for his endorsement deal?

REAL ESTATE: LARGEST ASSET CLASS IN THE WORLD

Real estate is often regarded as one of the safest asset classes. It is also the largest and a core component of almost every portfolio, whether in the form of homeownership, investment properties, or indirect stakes via trust vehicles. Apartment blocks, houses, shopping centers, office towers, hotels, warehouses—they are everywhere. We see, touch, smell, shop in, and live in real estate. When an asset class is tangible, the human psyche is more assured, akin to the certainty of possessing physical gold.

This brings to mind a quote from the 2006 movie *Inside Man*, spoken by "fixer" Madeleine White (played by Jodie Foster) during a bank heist: "You know, there's a famous saying by the Baron de Rothschild: 'When there's blood in the streets, buy property.'"

All words of wisdom require some qualification. Baron de Rothschild would certainly not have been a happy man if he had indiscriminately bought office property or physical retail shops in recent years. Post-COVID, remote working has become much more common, which has a material adverse effect on the overall demand for office space, especially if it is of subpar quality or location. In addition, the proliferation of online shopping, combined with rapid improvement in delivery capabilities, is causing a slow demise of lower-tier shopping centers, which continue to see thinning crowds.

Property value stems from actual and anticipated usage in the present and future, not the past. If demand for an office or retail space diminishes over time, it will command less lifetime rental, and valuation will drop. In contrast, a well-appointed single-family home in a good location will retain or enhance its value if it remains desirable.

Homeownership

Homeownership should be the cornerstone of any personal investing journey because owning one's home is more than just a financial decision. It can represent emotional stability, physical sanctuary, creative freedom, and independence. Homeownership serves a unique purpose for every personality type, whether it is the personal pride of a Type Nine peacemaker or a sense of achievement for the Type Three performers. There are, however, standard guardrails to observe, including limitations of affordability and parameters of due diligence to avoid overpaying—especially for the more impulsive personalities.

Real Estate Investment Trusts

The Empire State Building in New York City is one of the most recognizable buildings in the world. It is a cultural icon featured in many famous movies, including *Sleepless in Seattle* (1993) and *King Kong* (1933, 2005). The building is valued at over $2 billion, but we do not have to be Bill Gates to own it since this prized asset has belonged to the Empire State Realty Trust since 2014.

Empire State Realty Trust is an example of a real estate investment trust (REIT) publicly listed on the New York Stock Exchange. REITs own income-producing real estate, ranging from apartment blocks and warehouses to office and retail properties. Investors obtain indirect ownership of real estate portfolios when they purchase REIT units, just as with buying stocks on exchanges. In well-developed markets, REITs have special tax statuses that require rental income—after deducting expenses, fees, and interest payments—to be substantially distributed as dividends to shareholders. Owning REITs is an effective way to increase real estate allocation in any portfolio without having to purchase these big-ticket assets directly. One also gains income diversification when buying a REIT, as rental streams are usually spread across multiple tenancies.

The REIT market is divided into different property classes and geographies. Host Hotels & Resorts, for example, is a REIT that only invests in hotels, while Empire State Realty Trust is more diversified across office, retail, and multifamily, though the latter also focuses on assets located in Manhattan and the greater New York metropolitan area. Each segmentation comes with distinct risk factors, and it is vital to be aware of them. Since public REITs are traded on stock exchanges, their prices are subject to the same market forces, even though the underlying real estate asset valuation may not fluctuate with the same capriciousness.

Investment Properties

Investment properties are real estate assets purchased to generate income through rental or capital appreciation. The most common types of investment properties are residential, commercial (small office or retail units), and warehouses. Investors either purchase them individually or band together as a group to afford more significant assets.

A major advantage to owning real estate directly is the use of leverage at high loan-to-value ratios to make larger investments. Debt amplifies investment returns for property owners since interest and principal repayments are fixed (assuming that interest rates are predetermined) and investors retain any capital appreciation. Concurrently, one needs to be cognizant of downside risks. The 2008 global financial crisis resulted in many homeowners owing more on their mortgages than the values of their homes when the American economy collapsed and asset prices spiraled. Many property owners who took on more leverage to own multiple investment properties overextended their resources. When tenants terminated their leases for various reasons arising from economic hardship, servicing multiple mortgages without much of a cash buffer became impossible, leading to foreclosures and permanent investment losses.

Owning properties directly also comes with its fair share of maintenance costs. Actual physical structures depreciate over time; wear and tear can be a pain to handle and an expensive affair. Hiring property managers is an excellent way to deal with the nitty-gritty, though the additional cost of help will eat further into cash flow.

Ultimately, real estate investment requires patience. The key to investing in investment properties is to avoid overpaying in an overheated market and to stay liquid long enough to last through multiple cycles and disruptions, like vacancies, economic shocks, and repair work. Property owners should see a slow but robust payoff in the long run if rents move at least in tandem with inflation and asset valuation rises over time, local market conditions permitting.

STOCKS: HEADLINE GRABBERS

The most successful companies in the world are floated on major exchanges. There are exceptions, such as luxury brand Chanel and furniture giant IKEA, but almost all high-profile names are either listed entities (like 3M, Cheesecake Factory, Goldman Sachs, Boeing) or are owned by them, such as luxury brand Coach, owned by Tapestry, and LinkedIn, owned by Microsoft. Investors can therefore gain partial ownership in these big names by directly buying their stocks or indirectly by purchasing funds ranging from passive exchange-traded funds (ETFs) that replicate stock indices to mutual funds and active ETFs.

Money managers are incredibly creative when devising ways to assemble assortments of stocks and package them as thematic ETFs. In 2016, Janus Henderson Investors created the rather offensive-sounding "Obesity ETF" that invested in companies treating obesity and related health issues. That fund did not last long; it was shut down by early 2020.

Investors should note that they bear the cost of paying fund managers and their armies of analysts when investing in managed funds. Fees (measured by an expense ratio and expressed as a percentage of assets under management) are deducted from the value of pooled assets each year. On the other hand, there is no recurring cost involved in holding individual names and marginal fees when investing in passive ETFs.

Individual Stocks

100-Baggers is the title of a classic book written by Christopher Mayer. It is about looking for stocks that return a hundredfold, the kind of dream all long-term stock pickers yearn to make reality. Today, the most valuable companies in the world have performed better than a hundredfold, based on their initial public offering prices. To capture that level of investment returns, however, one must buy and hold a stock for a long time, enduring multiple market cycles, economic crises, wars, sanctions, bad earnings, analyst downgrades, and, most of all, endless self-doubt that arises with price choppiness.

The onus is on the investor to decide whether one is holding a

BlackBerry-equivalent company or the next Apple in the making. Often, this is apparent only in hindsight. When red flags show for an investment—and even Apple has demonstrated more than a few over its corporate life—does one continue to hold, double down, or drop it like it's hot? The answer is never straightforward.

Diversified Exchange-Traded Funds

The S&P 500 index is the world's most-watched basket of stocks. It is curated by Standard and Poor's, a leading rating agency, and it represents the largest 500 companies (with demonstrated profitability) listed in the US. Index composition changes only once every year. New companies that gain in market value and inflect into profitability replace those that do the opposite. Some of the oldest constituents include Berkshire Hathaway, Johnson & Johnson, and Coca-Cola.

Why is this index so important? First, it cuts across multiple sectors, from the old economy to the new, and across companies with varying growth profiles. Coca-Cola may not be growing at the same rate as the current big thing in the food and beverage industry, but consumers are still drinking Minute Maid juices (over seventy-five years of goodness) and Coke. Sheer diversification across 500 companies ensures that investors are not skewed toward or omitting any meaningful sector in the American economy, the largest and most developed in the world.

The all-important feature of investing in an index is automatic rebalancing, which mitigates the critical risk of investing in individual stocks: doubling down on losers and selling winners. Many investors find taking losses far more painful psychologically than cashing in gains so that we may keep the clunkers in our portfolios longer than justifiable. Or worse, we sell winners too soon to take profit and average down on losers. Therein lies the key advantage of an index. When one buys a unit in an S&P 500 index fund, that unit represents the latest 500 companies in the index. It keeps pace with all changes to index composition. The constituency is renewed based on objective measures, and there is no sentimentality. In other words, it takes away investor biases that can do more damage than good.

Thematic Funds

Thematic funds can run the gamut, from industry-specific (like financials, energy, and technology) and purpose-driven (sustainability-focused) to those that only invest in developing markets, European stocks, potential acquisition targets, undervalued stocks, or consistent dividend payers.

One of the most popular and topical themes in the fund management industry relates to environmental, social, and governance issues (ESG). In recent years, ESG has become ubiquitous at grassroots levels, from the food we consume ("Go vegan!") and the cars we drive ("Internal combustion engines are killing Mother Earth!") to the clothes we wear (recycling old outfits) and how we deal with food waste (composting, of course). By extension, many individual investors are also starting to vote with their dollars, creating opportunities for fund managers to create more thematic funds with ESG principles as central pillars to determine assets under management. Exchange-traded funds with ESG goals have hence become one of the hottest areas of finance, fusing the concept of low-cost ETFs tracking broad indices with sustainability considerations.

ESG funds can be put together in different ways. Some managers simply exclude companies that do not fit the definition of ESG or fall short on ratings provided by third-party agencies. Companies that deal with tobacco, fossil fuels, and gambling are almost always eliminated. Other ESG funds pick companies based on a mix of financial performance and external ratings to formulate individual constituencies. There are also ESG funds that are even more specific—for example, investing only in the renewable energy sector, companies with a track record of equal pay, or those that advance the electrification of vehicles.

A few things to note about ESG-focused funds: ESG rating

criteria can vary widely by agency, and subjectivity is involved. There is no global definition for each environmental, social, and governance criterion. When measuring employee satisfaction, are unionized workers happier than those who are not? Should Glassdoor ratings be used, or do agencies rely on what human resources commission to quantify employee relations? In 2022, the S&P ESG Index famously excluded Tesla but kept Exxon Mobil, an outcome that baffled many. Technology companies also tend to get heavier weights in such funds because they have little physical footprint; neither do they require heavy logistics to deliver software services. Hence, they score relatively well under the "E" part of ESG, and a typical result of investing in some ESG funds is an inadvertent skew toward the technology sector.

FIXED INCOME

Fixed income, as the name suggests, refers to investments that pay out a fixed amount of interest periodically. More creditworthy borrowers, like the US government, will therefore only pay minimal borrowing costs to lenders, while riskier ones—think developing countries and companies that have yet to stabilize operations to reach escape velocity—pay more interest.

Default risk is not the only consideration when investing in this asset class. Market values of fixed-income instruments, like all financial assets traded on open exchanges, can fluctuate wildly, especially with interest rate changes. Silicon Valley Bank famously went under in 2023, partly because the bank held large swaths of low-yielding treasuries that lost value in a rising interest rate environment. When they needed cash in order to satisfy sudden deposit withdrawals, the bank had to sell their fixed-income investments at substantial losses.

Fixed-income instruments issued by creditworthy institutions offer investors the preservation of capital and income, but only when they are held to maturity. Until then, their market values are subject to the whipsaws of market cycles. When investing via bond funds, investors may note that the same liquidity dynamics faced by Silicon Valley Bank can be replayed when fund managers handle unexpected redemptions by investors.

ALTERNATIVE INVESTMENTS

Here, alternative asset classes are those that do not fit into the above real estate, stocks, or fixed-income buckets. They can run the gamut, including commodities, art, gems, collectibles (like the 1960 No. 1 issue of *Justice League of America* comic book), venture capital, private equity, financial derivatives, and digital currencies. The term "alternative" may be a misnomer, as certain commodities like gold and diamonds are mainstream asset classes that have proven to retain or grow in value over time.

Perhaps no alternative investment has attracted more hype and speculation than cryptocurrencies in the twenty-first century. Since debuting in 2009, Bitcoin is by far the most common and popular digital currency. It even gained a degree of legitimacy in corporate America when companies like fintech giant Block and Tesla elected to hold Bitcoin on their balance sheets. If enough people decide that Bitcoin is the equivalent of gold sometime in the future, Bitcoin will gain more price stability and a place in conventional asset allocation. No one knows when that day will come and how much each Bitcoin will be worth in that scenario.

Alternative investments can be subject to extreme speculation and arbitrary pricing. Why is the *Balloon Dog* by artist Jeff Koons worth millions, while other creations sell for mere fractions in Bangkok's Chatuchak Weekend Market? Will the *Balloon Dog* hold its value 200 years from today, as old master paintings have? Who knows, but I wish I were Koons's early patron when he was still an unknown.

EVERYTHING EVERYWHERE, BUT NOT ALL AT ONCE

In the film *Everything Everywhere All at Once* (2022), the key characters inhibit multiple parallel universes simultaneously. It makes for a confusing watch, but the screen chaos does converge to tie up the storyline.

Asset allocation implies everything and everywhere, straddling disparate asset classes that lend a degree of stability to the whole. However, unlike Michelle Yeoh's character in the movie, we need not do it all at once. This is a lifelong process, not a two-hour race for emotional payback to win an Oscar. Mistakes in the past inform the present and future so that we can make multiple changes to our portfolios over market cycles.

We all have more than 139 minutes to reinvent ourselves and our asset allocations.

Chapter 3

Type One: Monica Geller (of *Friends*)

Remember *Friends* (1994-2004), the comedy sitcom from the 1990s? The premise is simple: It follows six distinctive (and attractive, of course) singles living in New York City and hanging out at the Central Perk café at all hours of the day. Trials and tribulations follow these six friends as they navigate budding careers, caricature parents, and dating lives. Throw in some sexual tension in the group, and you have a hit sitcom that ran for ten seasons over ten years. More than fifty million Americans watched the season finale in 2004, making it one of the most popular shows in television history.

During its ten-year run, the show successfully reached its target audience (the highly coveted eighteen-to-forty-nine-year-olds), which led to the flywheel effect of more advertising dollars and higher production budgets to keep the show going. *Friends* remains popular to this day. In 2015, more than ten years after the finale aired, Netflix paid north of $100 million for the streaming rights over several years. According to Nielsen, the show was consistently one of the most popular shows on the platform. Then, in 2019, HBO Max outbid Netflix with a price tag of $425 million to stream *Friends* exclusively for five years, starting in 2021.

How does a twenty-plus-year-old television show remain relevant to a new generation of fans? None of the characters even use Facebook,

Tinder, or iPhones. Why are modern audiences still relating to *Friends*?

A key reason for its enduring appeal may be how the six characters are written. Each is highly distinctive, and in aggregate, they cover six major personality archetypes that transcend time, geography, and culture. For example, some of us can relate to the intellectual Ross Geller, who is portrayed as a shy introvert but grows bolder to declare his love for Rachel Green. Others may resonate with Joey Tribbiani, an optimistic and outgoing actor with an adventurous personality. All six characters on the show get equal attention from the writers, and each friend has a well-developed backstory to provide further emotional depth. In other words, people connect with *Friends* beyond just the comedy: They see themselves in the characters.

Below are the likeliest Enneagram types for the six friends:

- Monica Geller (played by Courteney Cox): Type One (Perfectionist)
- Rachel Green (played by Jennifer Aniston): Type Three (Performer)
- Ross Geller (played by David Schwimmer): Type Five (Investigator)
- Chandler Bing (played by Matthew Perry): Type Six (Skeptic)
- Joey Tribbiani (played by Matt LeBlanc): Type Seven (Enthusiast)
- Phoebe Buffay (played by Lisa Kudrow): Type Nine (Peacemaker)

Of the six, Monica Geller is perhaps the easiest to label since her character portrayal is particularly over-the-top. A running gag on the show revolves around her obsession with cleaning. In one memorable scene, Monica cleans the body of her upright vacuum with a handheld one while expressing her wish for an even smaller version to clean the one she is holding. Before Marie Kondo normalized OCD-like behaviors, there was Monica Geller as a poster child for everyone who wants decorative pillows fluffed constantly and placed precisely where they should be.

Monica's strong Type One (perfectionist) personality, though coming across like a cartoon sometimes, is well constructed and consistent with other aspects of her character. Her profession culminates in a position as a high-end chef, a job that requires great attention to detail. Since childhood, Monica believes her parents favor her brother, Ross, and resents them for it. Judy Geller, her mother, is shown to be especially critical of Monica. Combined with childhood obesity, early feelings of inadequacy have led to her predisposition to chase perfection. From maintaining the impeccable condition of her apartment to planning Phoebe's wedding like a four-star general, Monica adheres to her standards and ideals in everything she does. The burden of perfection, however, can have unintended consequences. As reliable and steadfast as she is, Monica often finds herself at odds with her friends and colleagues over her intractable behavior.

PERSONALITY OF TYPE ONES (PERFECTIONISTS)

In real life, I reckon Monica Geller would not be pleasant company. Imagine having her over at your place and being made to feel like a slob as she judges your decor, organization, and whether you made your bed. Or worse, picture her as your mother. God help us all. She is a comic foil on the show, and it is funny only on television. Thankfully, most Type Ones do not behave in such extreme ways; few of us can be as insufferable as Monica Geller and still manage to retain lifelong friends.

Type Ones are typified by their drive for perfection. But what are the ideals that accompany this drive? They can range from religious principles and the law of the land to personal ethos and dietary habits. In other words, whatever these perfectionists believe to be the correct set of values is curated—consciously or unconsciously—over time, often in an arbitrary fashion. Type Ones are sticklers for their own rules, pushing themselves hard to be on the "right" side. In doing so, they often repress their inner urges and desires that do not comply with said standards. The pushier Type Ones will impose their beliefs on others, even as they struggle to uphold them.

Since Type Ones are part of the gut triad, they are driven by instinct. If these strict beings (or others around them) do not meet the ideals they hold dear, quick action—often fueled by anger over noncompliance—will be taken. Compared to Type Eights (challengers), who are assertive with people, and Type Nines (peacemakers), whose outward actions can be disconnected from their inner intuitions, Type Ones direct their energies inward to focus on what they must do.

Such activities can range from self-improvement to carrying out system-wide reforms. Think exercising strenuously to attain that "ideal" body, advocating for minority voices to be heard at the workplace, organizing placards to campaign against oil companies, and championing independence from colonial overlords. Unlike Monica Geller, most Type Ones do not go around washing dirty cars that do not belong to them or offering to clean a stranger's apartment just because it is an epic mess.

On the healthier end of the spectrum, Type Ones are principled individuals who aim for excellence but are unburdened by the concept of unattainable perfection. They are steadfast in their desire for self-improvement and yet gracious with contentment, without the self-reproach that stems from feelings of inadequacies. They do what they believe to be right and often inspire (rather than impose on) others to do the same. Because healthy Ones are realistic with the full range of humanity, including their own, not only do they accept differences of opinions and behaviors, but they do so with empathy, which makes them relatable and therefore even more influential. Healthy Type

Ones are conscientious and discerning yet free of rigid rules since their ideals are rooted in principles that adapt to changing realities.

In contrast, unhealthy Type Ones are intolerant of others who do not subscribe or conform to their ideals. They act like Bible thumpers, severe and aggressive yet full of sins themselves. Critical and judgmental, they do not possess grace for errors in themselves or others. Since nobody is perfect and everyone makes mistakes, anger (against self and others) accumulates in their bodies until it becomes rage.

So, we may have two Type One perfectionists, but if they are at different ends of the ego spectrum, they can come across as different people even as they espouse the same values. The ego-free version is likely experienced as an inspiration, someone who is moral without being moralistic and righteous without an air of self-righteousness. The unhealthy and egotistical Type One, on the other hand, will come across as dogmatic to the hilt.

CHECKLIST FOR TYPE ONE

If you respond "Yes" to, or resonate with, most of the questions and the statements below, you are likely to be a Type One:

- ☐ Organization and neatness come naturally to you, and you enjoy rolling up your sleeves to put everything in order, even during your free time.
- ☐ You are detail-oriented and will not hesitate to drill down to the nitty-gritty yourself, from using home appliances and compliance with tax filings to handling professional obligations at work.
- ☐ You pride yourself on adhering to your moral, religious, professional, ethical, and behavioral standards.

- ☐ "Good enough" is not enough. You feel compelled to make things properly right.
- ☐ When stressed, you sometimes wish to shed the burden of sticking to your standards and relax like everyone else.
- ☐ You have strong, almost visceral convictions on many aspects of your life, including political views, social injustices, how to be a good spouse, friendship 101, or dietary discipline.
- ☐ Good rules must be followed, and people should adhere to them to maintain order, but when rules do not make sense, you feel a strong urge to undertake reformative actions.
- ☐ You are your harshest critic and tend to beat yourself up when you make mistakes.
- ☐ When you see others flouting or disrespecting what you consider proper protocol, you feel angry toward them and almost want to teach them a lesson.
- ☐ You have an opinion on almost everything and want to make it known to others.

TYPE ONE INVESTORS

Of all Enneagram personality types, Type One investors care most about detail and do so with much enthusiasm. Despite belonging to the gut triad and possessing strong action biases, Type One investors may refrain from deploying capital until every investing detail lines up in accordance with their high standards. This creates a philosophical challenge since almost all investment activities entail uncertainties and ambiguities.

A desire for precision can become a hindrance and cause one to lose sight of the forest for the trees. Economist John Maynard Keynes once stated, "It is better to be roughly right than precisely wrong." The impulse to get details straightened out and polished is second nature to these perfectionists, but if left unchecked, it could misdirect energy to seeking exactness at the expense of taking action. Allowing the illusion of completeness to determine the course of investment actions—just because it checks all the boxes—can also lead an investor in precisely the wrong direction.

CORE MOTIVATION: TO MAKE IT RIGHT

Type Ones are systematic in their approach to everything, and when it comes to personal investing, Type One investors are built for the kind of intense due diligence that leaves no stones unturned. If a detailed rental and expense forecast model needs to be built before deciding on an investment property, I would want it done by Type One personalities. They will analyze and reanalyze with multiple sets of assumptions covering different scenarios, with conscientious precision.

While being methodical is essential for any investor, it can be taken too far when it becomes pedantic. What is deemed right is always subjective in personal investing. Is there ever a right valuation for a property? Or the right mix of sector exposure in portfolio construction? Does the definition of what is right change with time and circumstances? Are Type One investors prepared to amend or even forget what is right to fit changing realities?

PRIMARY INFATUATION: PERFECTION

"Perfection is the enemy of the good."

Investing is messy. We work with incomplete information before making decisions with our hard-earned dollars. Is Jensen Huang, cofounder of Nvidia, an excellent leader to bet on in the chip sector? Will Apple continue to dominate the consumer electronics market as the most profitable and coveted brand? Will American dollars remain the global currency of choice in the next fifty years? No one knows, and some information can never be pinned down, at least not for long before variables change again.

Leon Levy, the legendary investor and cofounder of Oppenheimer mutual funds, once said: "There is never perfect knowledge about the world. Simply put, we don't know what we don't know." That's a sentiment I'll be repeating a lot in the pages ahead. Are Type One investors prepared to accept such imperfect grounds and proceed based on probabilities?

Seeking perfection in investing—for example, gathering complete information, building the best possible financial model, checking off every investment criterion, and covering all downside cases—is futile. Perfection does not exist because everything has puts and takes that shift in the balance at every moment. Trying to ascertain too many variables can paralyze Type One investors.

KEY AVOIDANCE: MAKING MISTAKES

Many Type Ones crave ultraprecision and order because they do not wish to make mistakes. However, everyone makes them, so that mental refusal to accept the occurrence of error leads to anger—plenty of it. Ever wonder *why* those Bible thumpers are often so angry? That is because they cannot accept their own sins!

The real sin in personal investing is to avoid committing any. Investment outcomes are often beyond our control; to obsess over predictability is to limit investment choices. That rigidity may even prevent Type One investors from seeing obvious pitfalls because they are too engrossed in their quest for flawless investment theses.

It should be noted, however, that regardless of Enneagram types, none of us have an unlimited capacity to sustain endless blunders.

We are emotional creatures and demand the comfort of knowing our competencies. Moreover, to be wrong all the time when it comes to personal investing can wipe out resources and put a hard stop to everything. For Type One investors whose tolerance for missteps is even lower, tripping up on their financial journeys too fast too soon could put them off for good. In other words, a form of exposure therapy is needed to first acquaint them with volatility, but not so much that they throw in the towel prematurely.

Mistakes are unavoidable when investing. Nothing is a sure bet. The real error is to avoid making any bets at all.

CHIEF PROVOCATION: BEING CRITICIZED

If a Type One investor holds oneself to the highest standards of achieving alpha returns every single year, and a bear market ravages portfolio performance, that feedback loop will be received like a tormenting critic. And if anyone then tries to offer that Type One investor advice, good luck. Hell hath no fury like a Type One critiqued!

We all have our inner critics, and everyone has an element of perfectionism. For Type Ones, that inner critic is especially loud, and external criticism is amplified. They are hard on themselves already, and all their efforts are designed to avoid experiencing shortcomings. The instinctual fear is that they are not good enough, and anything that arouses that fear can provoke disproportionate reactivity. Hence, criticisms can be very challenging for Type One investors, especially when it is as unequivocal as negative percentage returns, over which they feel they have no control.

BLIND SPOT #1: RIGIDITY HINDERING THE INVESTING PROCESS

Being outcome-focused can be an incredible source of discipline and strength in personal investing. Obtain an industry report on recent hospitality trends before investing in the sector? Check. Generate property transactions in the last six months and run correlation analyses to ascertain the price to pay for an investment property? Done. Hire an industry expert to discuss competitive advantages and disadvantages that top cybersecurity service providers face as customers consolidate solutions on fewer platforms? Signed, sealed, delivered.

Type One investors stick to the rules of engagement and get energized by adherence. If following a methodology for investing gives them a sense of competence, then they will follow it to a tee. But that inelasticity can backfire. If no allowance is made for the unknown and everything needs to fit a set of predetermined scenarios, any slight deviation will result in internal distress. Inflexibility also limits the perceived range of available options. Can something be done in another way to get the same outcome? Absolutely. Must all due-diligence boxes be checked before proceeding with an investment opportunity? Definitely not.

Type One investors are prone to an all-or-nothing mindset due to their rigidity; counterbalancing with flexibility in thinking and doing is hence a dialectic challenge they must embrace.

BLIND SPOT #2: LOSING THE FOREST FOR THE TREES

Type Ones are prone to allowing checkboxes to take a life of their own. Just because an investment opportunity satisfies all their curated (and subjective) conditions does not mean that it is the greatest thing since sliced bread. Take value traps as an example. At any point, more than a few publicly traded companies—including some that are still constituents of major indices and owned by global investment funds—face existential crises. In America, the likes of cigarette makers or legacy technology giants that are unable to sustain product relevance are prime value traps. As a result, these companies tend to trade at depressed prices. While they may score high on calculated indicators (such as returns on invested capital, price-earnings ratios, and dividend yields), any long-term investment thesis built solely on the strength (and comforts) of these defined metrics is a significant impairment waiting to happen.

TYPE ONES:
WHEN DEALING WITH INVESTMENT SUCCESSES AND FAILURES

The quest for perfect investments may create inertia that can hinder success and enlarge failures for Type One investors.

When a so-called perfect investment that checks all the boxes is found, it can create an anchoring bias. Resistance to seeing shifting tides then becomes a significant risk. Maybe diamonds are forever, but almost all investments are subject to change, and success may not be sustained over long periods. External shocks can create disruptions that upend original investment theses. Bookstore chain Borders and video rental giant Blockbuster might have been one-time stars, but the digital revolution has made them almost irrelevant. Their demise was slow and painful. If either of them had qualified as an ideal investment, Type One investors might remain unwavering in their convictions far longer than if they were to acknowledge a margin of error in their analyses.

Successes and failures defined in simplistic binary do not allow space for experimentation. Type One investors, with their tendencies for self-reproach, may regard any investment that falls short as a failure rather than an inevitable mistake on a long investment journey. It need not be a total write-off, but disproportionate anger and frustration can still erupt if the performance does not meet their high expectations. Experiencing such emotional turmoil on an investing journey is exhausting, and it takes them away from extracting valuable lessons when investments do not pan out according to a script. If

Type Ones keep hearing the message of being "not good enough," the personal investing journey is neither sustainable nor healthy.

ROAD MAP FOR TYPE ONE INVESTORS

In general, Type One investors do not deal well with volatility. When paving their financial journeys, a minimum degree of predictability is essential to keeping Type One investors engaged and not enraged.

Think back to early 2020 when stock markets worldwide started to crumble under the weight of COVID-19 fears, with nonstop news of the impending apocalypse. How did Type One investors cope with that kind of messiness? Even stable, blue-chip stocks—Bank of America, Walmart, Coca-Cola, and the like—moved in tandem with the broader markets when volatility peaked. The psychological impact of witnessing portfolio valuations crash can have an adverse effect on mindset, especially for Type One investors who crave order.

Equities and any other volatile asset classes must not play a leading role in a Type One investor's journey. Neither should they be featured in early scenes. Instead, the portfolio focus should be on tangible assets that do not have Bloomberg and CNBC tracking their exact values from one microsecond to the next.

HOMEOWNERSHIP AS A FIRST INVESTMENT ASSET

Owning real estate for Type One perfectionists is, well, perfect. As owner-occupiers, Type Ones are naturally motivated to keep their homes in spotless condition, aligning every cushion and wiping out all irregularities. Every appliance is kept in its best working condition because all regular maintenance works will be carried out at optimal and precise intervals. No wall crack will be left unattended; no stove will be left unpolished. All things being equal, properties owned by Type Ones are far more likely to be better maintained and their values protected.

The first home my husband and I purchased was flawlessly presented when we first surveyed the house. Every item was where it should be, down to the exact organization of dish towels and labeling of gift-wrapping supplies in a remote closet. The previous owners must have been disciples of Marie Kondo. Recognizing their Type One perfectionistic fingerprints everywhere and knowing the property must have been well maintained, we felt comfortable proceeding with the purchase, even at a slight premium.

Real estate is an essential component of any retirement portfolio, and it is best suited for those who appreciate and care for it the way Type Ones do. Renting is inevitable at the start of one's career and likely the only option, apart from crashing at someone else's place or inheriting a space from a rich relative. The focus, however, should be to save up toward a down payment for a home as soon as practicable by minimizing rental payments. Forget the "rule" that one should afford rent up to x percent of take-home salary; Type One investors should work backward based on how much they should save each month toward purchasing their first homes within the shortest possible time frame.

AMASS INVESTMENT RESIDENTIAL PROPERTIES

By extension, residential investment properties should also be part of a Type One investor portfolio. Managing such assets will be a cinch: Type Ones go the extra mile to ensure that their properties stand out from the competition, with meticulous attention paid to everything from choosing the right filters for marketing photographs to staging the premises with plants, art pieces, and even scented candles to wow prospective tenants and buyers.

Type One investors are suited to accumulating and managing residential units, whether to rent out or resell after extensive makeovers.

Although the process—from hunting for suitable properties to renovation, marketing, and all the paperwork—may sound daunting to many, Type One investors are likelier to enjoy the challenge than be put off. Their natural flair for organizing, fixing imperfections, and tying loose ends gives them a sustainable edge in accumulating and managing such assets in the long run.

Type One landlords will require some external help—handypersons, agents, stagers—at some point, but not everyone fits the bill. Since detail is of the utmost importance, Type Ones will work best with third parties who are also Type One perfectionists. Otherwise, the delegation process could degenerate quickly into the dark side of micromanagement.

CONSIDER ALTERNATIVE TANGIBLE INVESTMENTS

Perhaps no other Enneagram type appreciates precise workmanship and painstaking handiwork better than Type One perfectionists. Art, artifacts, and jewelry may resonate with Type One investors; they have proven excellent investments for the discerning. Imagine owning a Jean-Michel Basquiat painting from the 1980s, when he was an unknown artist. The point is, if a Type One investor enjoys such possessions and accumulating knowledge thereof, they can add interesting diversification (and potentially enhance overall returns) to one's investment portfolio.

AVOID INDIVIDUAL STOCKS AND SPECULATIVE ASSETS

If profits can be made from trading ownership, technology will enable it. Everything from bushels of corn to a nonfungible token created out of Jack Dorsey's first-ever tweet can be purchased online. Stocks still grab the most headlines, and the idea of hunting for the next-generation Nike or Walt Disney is seductive to many. Unless a Type One investor is uniquely qualified to invest in a particular company due to in-depth academic or professional know-how, it is best to obtain exposure to equities via index funds (see paragraph below for more detail). Stock picking often introduces more volatility than what Type One investors can endure, given their penchant for order and structure. Speculative assets, especially cryptocurrencies and anything metaverse-related, are even more volatile and must be avoided, no matter how many investors jump on the bandwagons. While there is no hiding from the chaos of globalized markets, some pockets can and should be excluded by Type One investors.

DIVERSIFICATION WITH INDEX FUNDS

While investing in specific stocks is not recommended, participating in a regular investment plan that provides Type One investors with equity and fixed-income exposures via index funds is essential for diversification. This should be undertaken after homeownership and only in small quantities at the start; Type One investors should feel secure in a portfolio anchored in a large tangible asset before adding more volatile asset classes to the mix. Even if markets turn bearish, they will not move the needle in the early stages of this diversification exercise.

PERFORM PORTFOLIO REVIEWS WITH THIRD PARTIES

It is easy to get lost in detail and forget the bigger picture. For example, a Type One investor may obsess over the choice of paint color for a rental apartment after a vacancy spell, but the better decision to contemplate may be whether to sell the property and recycle capital elsewhere. The ability to step back and think strategically without getting overwhelmed by the details is essential to ensure course correction before it is too late. Type One investors can benefit from seeking alternative perspectives from third parties since they tend to get tangled in the weeds.

Engaging professional advisers (such as real estate agents, financial advisers, consultants, and industry experts) provides a valuable gut check when doing periodic reviews of one's financial health. It should be noted, however, that Type Ones tend to be rather headstrong and can be argumentative when opinions do not conform to theirs. Worse, they may try to convince their advisers to tell them what they want to hear. Slowing down to practice active listening is critical; perhaps of equal importance is hiring nonpliant, firm advisers who will hold their own in the face of Type Ones.

DEVELOPMENT PLAN FOR ONES: INTEGRATING TOWARD TYPE SEVEN (ENTHUSIAST) AND TYPE FOUR (INDIVIDUALIST)

The closing scene from the 2010 film *Black Swan* is haunting and dramatic. Lead character Nina Sayers (played by Natalie Portman) delivers a searing performance in the production of *Swan Lake* but succumbs to her self-inflicted injuries as she utters her final words: "I felt it . . . it was perfect."

It is a role to die for—literally. Sayers yearns for perfection and exercises tremendous discipline to achieve it. In one memorable scene early in the movie, her artistic director, Leroy, dismisses her rigor: "Perfection is not just about control. It's also about letting go. Surprise yourself so you can surprise the audience. Transcendence."

Sayers does achieve transcendence in the end, after embracing her darker self, but at great cost.

The story presents a somber look into the quest for perfection. Some people search for their dream spouses (on Hinge or in real life); others aim for that ideal job or a flawless body shape. Happiness becomes correlated with the attainment of lofty objectives. The urge to stick that perfect landing is even more compelling for Type Ones.

When that mission overtakes all consciousness, it becomes myopic. Sayers is so blinded by her focus on playing the lead role in *Swan Lake* that she does not realize the emotional, mental, and physical anguish she is putting herself through.

Development for Type Ones (perfectionists) is indeed letting go, as described by Leroy in the movie. In Enneagram speak, it refers to embracing two key pivots that are critical to resetting focus. Type Sevens (enthusiasts) present one such direction: They embody the essence of letting go and relaxing into the whole experience of being present. Rather than being constrained by rules, real or imagined, Type Seven enthusiasts go big on living up to their visions. Perfection or strict adherence to standards need not be a prerequisite to action; Type Sevens demonstrate that a good dose of enthusiasm is all we need to move forward. Rather than waiting for all the stars to align or being held back by concerns of whether they are good enough, Type Ones can relax into accepting what is, thus freeing up their energies to pursue more interests and embrace their inner playfulness. Type Seven enthusiasts epitomize that spontaneous and experiential approach to learning. Self-flagellation is not necessary to become better.

Type Fours (individualists) present another direction. The title *Black Swan* refers to the negative other of White Swan—a side embodied by the character Lily, a free-spirited dancer whom Sayers both fears and envies. The liberated and sexual side personified by Lily is one that Sayers rejects her whole life because it taints her concept of being perfect. Yet it is a side that she—and the audience—must ultimately confront. We only see her freed at the end when she finally accepts her inner White Swan and Black Swan in equal measure. Humans possess lightness and darkness; denying the bad is equivalent to repression. The more we try to subdue a trait, the worse it rears its ugly head. It is much healthier to acknowledge every part of ourselves with grace while working on becoming more than just a binary. We can be good people with the capacity to improve while still retaining every flaw, urge, and deficiency. All elements can evolve together. The most effective antidote to the Type One repressive nature is hence a Type Four archetype. Like Lily in the film, Type Fours are not afraid to express themselves, along with all the highlights and lowlights of their beings.

Order and chaos can coexist because they do in the real world of investing. The challenge for Type One investors is to get comfortable with dialectical states, deriving mental comfort from having the skill set to instill self-discipline and simultaneously accept the unpredictable. All any investor can do to reduce systematic risks is hold a diversified portfolio with a mix of asset classes of different risk profiles. When Type One perfectionists stop expending so much energy trying to control every outcome and accept the unknown to enjoy the process of personal investing, they will have achieved transcendence.

Chapter 4

Type Two:
Katherine Johnson (of *Hidden Figures*)

Hidden Figures is a 2016 biographical film about African American mathematicians—all female—who worked at NASA during the years of the Space Race. Before the advent of computers, these women were employed as human computers to perform calculations by hand. Due to segregation policies, they were required to work in a separate building called the West Area Computers.

The movie focuses on three main characters—Katherine Johnson, Mary Jackson, and Dorothy Vaughan—who are outstanding employees but struggle for equal opportunities due to their skin color. It is a story of how each of the three ladies fights her way out of being kept hidden in the woodwork to get her due credit. With that in mind, the title *Hidden Figures* has a dual meaning, referring to the unheralded but essential mathematical work behind each test flight and how segregation policies relegated these characters to the background.

Arguably, the most brilliant of the three women is Katherine Johnson, portrayed by Taraji P. Henson as gifted, hardworking, and collegial. Because of her specific skills in analytic geometry, Johnson is recruited by NASA's Space Task Group, a working team of engineers under pressure to put an American in orbit after the Soviet Union has succeeded with Yuri Gagarin on board Vostok 1. As the only African

American in the Space Task Group, she works extra hard to prove herself. Johnson is dedicated to her country's mission to win the Space Race, even if it means playing second fiddle to peers (all White men) who are far less capable and diligent.

Female and Black, Johnson faces discriminatory treatment from her colleagues, from the juvenile exclusion from her share of fresh coffee to leaving her name out of reports she writes. The most poignant subplot involves bathroom access. Even with her equal credentials—and more than equal share of responsibility—Johnson is not allowed to use any White-only facilities in the building. She must walk (or run) half a mile back to the West Area Computers to relieve herself. She does not complain and even brings work into the stall to make up for lost time. Not only is Johnson receiving less pay than her White counterparts, but her basic needs are also not met. Yet she carries on without complaints.

Until she cannot anymore.

In a pivotal scene, when the head of the Space Task Group notices her frequent absences (due to bathroom needs) and accuses Johnson of being irresponsible, she finally breaks down and calls out the abuses. This marks a turning point in the film, with Johnson summoning the courage to let out her brewing anger without fear. It also heralds the beginning of her character finally getting due credit. Instead of suffering in silence, Johnson becomes more assertive, pushing for a seat at the table during high-level meetings, putting her name on the cover of reports, and demonstrating her mathematical skills to a room full of high-ranking officials to calculate landing coordinates.

At the end of the film, Johnson takes a permanent position on the Space Task Group, and her contributions are fully recognized.

The film's portrayal of Katherine Johnson shows an archetypal Type Two (giver). Her home life further emphasizes her characterization: As a widow with three daughters, Johnson works hard to provide for them and still plays the role of a doting mother when she is home. In other words, she is someone who puts others before herself.

Yet the path toward self-development for Type Twos requires a different stroke: to put themselves first. In the film, Katherine Johnson attains true fulfillment when she takes up space to fight for her own professional (and personal) happiness.

PERSONALITY OF TYPE TWOS (GIVERS)

Type Twos are people-oriented and place high importance on relationships, from family and friends to professional associates and colleagues. They are giving personalities motivated to extend a helping hand; hence Type Twos are also known as "givers," "helpers," and "pleasers." There lies a strong correlation between self-esteem and the quality (or quantity) of relationships. Thinking and feeling patterns tend to move in tandem with how much Type Twos feel loved and appreciated for their acts of generosity. Such quid pro quo is often unconscious. As part of the heart triad with an outward focus, many rely on external appreciation to shape their emotional landscape.

Many Type Twos spread cheerfulness wherever they go. Coupled with their flair for reading emotions—in others more so than in themselves—a Type Two giver can pay compliments that hit all the right spots. They are also good listeners, happy to lend anyone a shoulder to cry on. In other words, this personality type is as close to a cheerleader-therapist combo as one can get.

At work, Type Twos enjoy taking on responsibilities and feeling useful in group projects. With excellent interpersonal skills, these giving beings are popular coworkers. They thrive on getting involved in teamwork and cultivating relationships. Often, they end up being friends with their colleagues outside of work. As leaders, the best Type Twos are empathetic and compassionate.

It is thus easy to see Type Twos as a hybrid between Wonder Woman and the idealized version of Mother Teresa—selfless to a fault. But this is not a realistic expectation. Even the most exceptional givers have their personal agendas. In fact, healthy Type Twos are in harmony with their own needs, neither ignoring nor denying them. Instead of trying to be the selfless superhero to win everyone over, the best Type Twos are just as honest and courageous in fighting for themselves. Recall Katherine Johnson becoming more assertive toward the second half of *Hidden Figures*: She is unabashed in pressing for individual recognition. Only when Johnson begins to stand up for herself does she demonstrate her true value to NASA and attain greater personal satisfaction.

On the other end of the spectrum, unhealthy Type Twos deny their own needs for fear of alienation or shame. To demonstrate anything outside of absolute goodness and selflessness is incongruent with public acceptance, so tending to individual goals (whether professional, social, financial, or emotional) conflicts with their self-image. Needless to say, no one can be selfless and good all the time. Prolonged repression combined with self-deceit leads to perversion of the intent behind their actions. These unhealthy givers resort to giving to get, demanding to be acknowledged as virtuous rather than being virtuous. An unspoken price tag is attached to their sacrificial deeds, and this can feel manipulative. A martyr complex propels their desire to be seen as modern-day Jesus Christs, dispensing unsolicited advice and assistance in their unconscious desire for external validation.

Because the methods to meet their needs are circuitous and disingenuous, frustration brews when unhealthy Type Twos do not receive the specific paybacks they expect. Worse, they may even double down on their bribes for recognition, which never seems enough. This often leads to biblical outbursts of anger. Never is a Type Two more selfish than when desperate to be seen as a gift to humankind.

CHECKLIST FOR TYPE TWO

If you respond "Yes" to, or resonate with, most of the questions and the statements below, you are likely to be a Type Two:

- ☐ Even when you feel down, you still have the energy to help others because it brings you immediate satisfaction.
- ☐ At work, you focus more on relationships with coworkers and team responsibilities than your individual checklists or tasks for the week.
- ☐ Detecting the moods, thoughts, and emotions in others comes easily to you, and you always know what to say to people.
- ☐ You are openly affectionate with family, friends, and even people you have just met to demonstrate your fondness for them.
- ☐ Charitable causes tug at your heartstrings, and you tend to donate more than your peers.
- ☐ You like having company and believe others enjoy yours too.
- ☐ In a work environment, you often take on more than your fair share of responsibilities because you feel personally obligated to do so rather than doing it to improve your career advancement or professional image.
- ☐ "Helpful" and "giving" are two of the most common adjectives people use to describe you.

- ☐ Professionally, you may be drawn to jobs or responsibilities that support broader economic, social, political, or environmental causes.
- ☐ Knowing that you have made a fundamental difference to people in your life gives you joy.

TYPE TWO INVESTORS

In theory, a Type Two may experience a conflict between wanting to be altruistic and identifying with the mission of personal investing. On the one hand, a giver is invested in what others need or want; in fact, most Type Twos are more attuned to people around them than to their inner selves. On the other hand, being an effective investor can be perceived as self-serving, an individualistic pursuit of one's financial goals. To a Type Two, the subject of money may be regarded as taboo, inspiring guilt and self-condemnation. How does one reconcile Mother Teresa with Wall Street?

The two objectives need not be mutually exclusive with the proper context and a mindset shift away from polarized perceptions of good and bad.

CORE MOTIVATION: TO BE SAVIORS

Superman has a compulsion to save the world, even if it means paying for it with his own life. Type Two investors may operate with the same script minus the power to return from the dead. Such a tendency can place them in compromising positions regarding finances. They may find it hard to say no when approached by friends or family for loans or capital to seed their businesses. Proposals like rescue financing—especially if they involve the kind of corporations that Type Twos feel sentimental toward—may resonate more with their emotions than merited.

When COVID-19 hit, many businesses had to raise cash to tide them through difficult times. Royal Caribbean and Carnival undertook several equity and debt financing rounds when cruises were canceled. Large and small theater chains resorted to various forms of fundraising, from grassroots-led campaigns to AMC Entertainment engineering a meme stock phenomenon to rally retail investors against short sellers. Type Two investors may be drawn to such calls out of an urge to be saviors.

While there is nothing wrong with wanting to support friends, family, and local businesses, this giving tendency becomes a problem when boundaries between investment merits and emotions are blurred. Are Type Two investors doing their part for charity to be good citizens or making investments with implicit expectations of returns? Another valid question to consider is intent. Is it possible that certain Type Two investors are positioning themselves as white knights, even when doing so may jeopardize their financial positions? Do they secretly seek out situations in which they are financially needed to feed their hungry hearts?

PRIMARY INFATUATION: RELATIONSHIPS

While personal investing can and should involve multiple other parties—including financial advisers or planners, bankers, friends, spouses, and other family members—the risk to Type Two investors is having too many cooks in the kitchen. Rather than asserting their objectives, they allow relationships with multiple parties to muddle the picture. Should they purchase an endowment policy from a particular friend to help him out? If an aunt is a financial planner, should a Type Two investor appoint her, even if someone else is more qualified or suitable?

A mix of disconnect from their individual needs and the innate desire to feel indispensable may expose Type Two investors to additional pitfalls. They can become a pawn in someone else's agenda. Whether or not these financial moves work out is a separate matter. The issue is losing their sense of agency relating to money decisions that should be made based on how fruitful those decisions are, not how much the Type Two wishes to feel of services to others.

Unhealthy Type Two investors are also susceptible to flattery. Persuading them to part with their cash thus becomes an exercise of emotional puppetry. Unless they have the financial savvy to hold firm to their own opinions, Type Two investors may fall prey to schemes that play to their heartstrings since the ability to identify downside scenarios and detect malice also becomes compromised.

KEY AVOIDANCE: SELF-SERVICE

Iconic character Gordon Gekko of *Wall Street* (1987) says greed is good. No other Enneagram type will find this statement more distasteful than Type Twos. They pride themselves on being noble people who like to help others and develop meaningful relationships. Self-enrichment is analogous to a virus invading the immune system: It feels wrong and needs to be purged. An inward look at one's own fiscal needs feels awkward. They may avoid planning for their financial future altogether, preferring to focus more on their jobs (to service their employers) and relationships with people. When left unchecked, they relinquish personal responsibility over their finances while obsessing over the affairs of others.

CHIEF PROVOCATION: LACK OF APPRECIATION

All humans want to be heard and feel valued for their gestures, opinions, feelings, and instincts. As giving and generous Type Two investors can be, they want and need to see returns, whether they admit it or not. Even if what they offer is an unequivocal gift, Type Twos still need to feel they are making an impact for reasons they care about, whether it is to mentor someone, campaign for political causes, or advance research into finding a cure for cancer.

When it comes to investing, financial returns—not just goodwill or appreciation—must be the measure of success. Investing is a business decision, not an act of charity, and Type Two investors should resist the temptation to equate financial contributions with emotional validation. When investments fail to perform and appreciate in value, it can understandably provoke negative emotions. Type Two investors need to realize that it is okay to feel disappointment; it does not signify unacceptable greed. Repressing or denying those emotions will only make it worse. Type Two investors are better off observing their feelings to uncover mistakes made and derive learning moments from them.

BLIND SPOT #1: REPRESSION OF INDIVIDUAL GOALS

We learn most of our coping mechanisms from childhood. Unless we are conscious of them, they tend to govern our adult behaviors in unconscious ways. Growing up, Type Two givers develop a belief that they must prioritize the needs of others above theirs; otherwise, punishment or karma may befall them. Without being encouraged to express their desires, they lose touch with who they are on the inside. An outward focus develops, and individual goals begin to feel like a foreign language. Consequently, hopes and dreams get repressed.

BLIND SPOT #2: INNER STRENGTH TO PURSUE OWN AGENDA

When focusing on others serves as a distraction from having to stare at one's own issues, avoidance becomes problematic. Unhealthy Type Twos become self-avoidant when they believe—consciously or unconsciously—that they do not have any problems or needs. Without exercising those muscles to fight their battles, Type Twos forget they possess the same human spirit that can do so much more than just follow the lead of others. We can all forge our paths and still enjoy healthy, interdependent relationships without codependency. In other words, we can simultaneously stand alone and with others. That inner strength is within all of us, and we must believe it.

When it comes to money, unhealthy Type Twos may not want to know how close or far along they are to building their financial safety nets, partly because they may not possess sufficient self-confidence. They turn outward because they are used to doing that, but that automatic response takes them further away from building financial savvy.

TYPE TWOS:
WHEN DEALING WITH INVESTMENT SUCCESSES AND FAILURES

A key issue with many Type Two investors is a missing North Star. Unhealthy Type Twos often develop an inadvertent fixation on others' investment road maps instead of their own. As a result, they are at risk of being disconnected from the ability to process their investing successes and failures.

If a Type Two investor happens to make an excellent real estate investment—say, a home that has had considerable appreciation—and a close friend or relative suggests taking out an equity loan to invest in a business, the chance of acquiescence is disproportionately high despite the potential risks involved. Because Type Twos are inclined to do others a favor, protecting their assets is critical to their financial stability.

Losses may be a different story. Type Two investors may suffer in silence and stuff their feelings when things go south, without taking remedial actions. They may ask for help, but most likely only from those they have done favors for in the past. As a result, the people they approach may not be suited to solve the problem. When unhealthy Type Twos feel dejected and rejected, they may devolve into frustration and hurt, creating a victim complex.

Unhealthy Type Two investors may also see themselves as having the purest of intent, so they walk away from taking personal responsibility. Expecting exoneration from others is equally likely. Because they are overly invested in being perceived as good people, mistakes that expose their weaknesses (especially blind spots, fixations, biases, misconceptions, and unhealthy coping mechanisms) are glossed over. No self-reflection transpires as a result, and Type Two investors miss out on valuable lessons that can only be learned through stumbles.

Whether success means achieving alpha returns or having peace of mind is subjective. There is no right or wrong answer. Investors still need to define their financial objectives first. Without a clear understanding of one's own investment goals, the picture of success or failure becomes ambiguous. How can one assess performance when there are no clear metrics against which to measure? Perhaps the lack of specific goals is also due to low self-confidence. That can become a catch-22 for Type Two investors.

ROAD MAP
FOR TYPE TWO INVESTORS

For Type Two investors, individual needs and desires can be unexpressed, under-expressed, or unconscious. Teasing out hidden feelings and thoughts cannot be done in a single meeting with a financial adviser. Neither would questionnaires on risk assessment help much. Type Twos have learned repression from a young age; even initial versions of their investment goals may need to be revised.

For this reason, freestyle writing is recommended as a first step to formulating a path forward because it will help Type Twos better connect to their inner selves. Consistent and prolonged scribing allows stream of consciousness to flow. By codifying their thoughts on paper (or screen), Type Two investors will better understand who they are and what they want.

Detailing a vision that resonates and inspires is a fundamental first step to financial planning for a Type Two investor. It does not matter how radical that vision may seem; it only needs to be meaningful to the Type Two individual and provide sustainable motivation to stay on course, minus guilt or shame. It is also essential to contextualize specific investment goals with societal and family elements so that Type Two investors can reconcile their emotions with a purpose larger than themselves.

CREATE A VISION BOARD

A good old vision board that represents what is important can further crystallize a Type Two's personal agenda. In addition to freestyle writing, vision boards can refocus Type Twos on achieving for themselves rather than others. Assembling a collection of images or objects helps to manifest latent desires and stir up inspiration for this heart triad type.

There is no limit to what Type Two investors should put on their vision boards. Working parents with children want to send them to specific colleges? Represent that with pictures of said institutions. A young couple dreams of a rustic-themed wedding with price tags closer to that of a St. Regis presidential suite than a random barn? Why not? We only live and marry once (hopefully).

The idea is to mold the mindset by bringing hopes and dreams to the foreground. An evocative vision board serves as a constant reminder of individual priorities. Whenever a financial decision needs to be made, the vision board is there to nudge Type Twos in the right direction. Beyond financial goals, vision boards can also include career aspirations, self-care, relationship ideals, and more.

HOMEOWNERSHIP AS A FAMILY RESPONSIBILITY

Homeownership to a Type Two should be viewed as a top personal responsibility, ensuring a permanent roof over one's head that is not subject to the whims of landlords or rental fluctuations. For Type Twos with young families, this may establish a sense of security for their children. So long as the choice of home is grounded and the selection well researched, homeownership is one of the most straightforward investments for anyone to make. Mortgage payments build equity over time and act as guardrails against excessive generosity.

FOCUS ON PASSIVE INVESTING VIA INDEX FUNDS

For Type Two investors, the natural inclination toward active management of personal stock portfolios will not be as strong as that of the take-charge Type Eight challengers, the competitive Type Three performers, or the cerebral Type Five investigators. Type Two givers are far more people-oriented and less competitive by nature, hence more suited to passive investing or tapping into the services of professional investment firms.

Automated contributions to retirement plans and index funds (stocks and fixed income) are easy to implement and forget. The exact monthly, quarterly, or annual amounts should be adjusted to adapt to changing financial circumstances. A regular investment plan takes advantage of dollar-cost averaging, removes the burden of market timing, and, more importantly, allows Type Twos to place their focus elsewhere without feeling like they have turned to the dark side of capitalism. Money is still put to work without causing too much cognitive dissonance to Type Two investors.

AVOID INDIVIDUAL STOCKS AND SPECULATIVE ASSETS

It is easy to get swept up in meme stocks, cryptocurrencies, and the current thing in the investment zeitgeist, especially if close friends or family members are also jumping on board. A desire to feel included may prompt Type Two investors to do the same. Chatter on the internet can quickly coalesce popular opinions around the hottest assets (the term "asset" is used loosely here) and bid up prices in public markets. Prices also tend to ratchet downward just as swiftly when sentiments shift. Unless a Type Two investor has specific knowledge that gives them clear information advantages, it is far better to stay away.

CAUTION ON INTERESTED PARTY TRANSACTIONS

When meaningful sums of money are involved with interested parties, especially relatives and close friends, Type Twos must observe their emotions and erect guardrails before making decisions. If deemed necessary to proceed, Type Two investors should clarify their own intentions. Is it a gift without expectation of return or repayment? If that is the case, the question becomes whether they can afford the generosity. Not every giver can afford to give; individual well-being should not suffer in the effort to be a good friend or family member.

When investing with interested parties, it is always better to document them as loans with conversion options versus pure equity. The former provides full principal repayment rights while retaining the option to convert into equity should the underlying business take off. Also, Type Two investors should seek advice from professional advisers or financially qualified individuals to get second opinions before proceeding. The odds of losing every penny are real, and Type Two investors need to be aware of both the risks and rewards when investing.

CONTINUALLY UPDATE VISION AND GOALS

Type Two investors must first develop a clear, inspiring vision to motivate them through the steps necessary to reach financial goals that resonate. Since investing is a lifelong journey, that vision should be refreshed regularly to provide enduring motivation. To kick-start their financial journeys, Type Two investors at the cusp of their careers may frame early objectives based on repayment of student loans (or other forms of expensive borrowings) and allocations to emergency funds. As life circumstances change, Type Two investors need to update their aspirations. The more precise and relevant the vision, the more motivated a Type Two investor will be to pursue congruent plans that continue to inspire.

SEEK PROFESSIONAL ADVICE TO ATTAIN VISIONS

Everyone needs—and deserves—quality help. We do not know everything, and we can all use a helping hand or a different perspective sometimes. Type Two givers need to acknowledge the same, even if they are used to giving. Disinterested but qualified third parties should be considered rather than simply turning to immediate friends or family members they feel comfortable with. Type Two investors should take the time to have their financial situations assessed by objective professionals. Such reality checks can yield valuable insights into what must be done to stay on course.

DEVELOPMENT PLAN FOR TWOS: INTEGRATING TOWARD TYPE FOUR (INDIVIDUALIST) AND TYPE EIGHT (CHALLENGER)

Many movies glorify epic heroes as fearless warriors always

prepared to die in service. Superman in *Batman v Superman: Dawn of Justice* (2016) risks his vulnerabilities by wielding a kryptonite spear to attack Zod, perishing in battle to save the world. Jack Dawson in *Titanic* (1996) freezes to death so that Rose DeWitt Bukater may live. Love is measured by loss, which further romanticizes ideations of self-sacrifice for Type Twos.

In the real world, no one needs to die for someone to live in every scenario. Self-sacrifice must not be the default starting point to earn love; we need to be more resourceful than the characters playing dramatic zero-sum games in movies. When everyone wins, the result is almost always healthier relationships with others and the self. This is in no way an invalidation of the great sacrifices that many real-life heroes have made to shape the world we know today. Instead, it is a reminder for Type Twos to consider their well-being as much as they consider that of others. Giving should feel like a choice, not the only option to earn love or a compulsive exchange to be loved.

The concept of what constitutes a good human being needs clarification. We all have individual needs, and they can take precedence. This is not being selfish. Just like plane passengers are always instructed to don their oxygen masks in emergencies before helping others, Type Twos must first take care of themselves. We are of much greater assistance to others when our own affairs are in order. Caretakers will feel more fulfilled when they stand on solid ground of their own. Personal happiness must come from within and be independent of external opinions. No outward acknowledgment will ever be enough to fill their inner voids.

With such an outward focus on the needs of others, it is no wonder that the two pivots toward personal development for givers are the introspective Type Four (individualist) and the dynamic Type Eight (challenger). Both provide necessary counterbalances. Leaning more into introspection allows the time and space to explore one's inner landscape. The key here is for Type Twos to be comfortable with being authentic, even when they detect inner darkness. We all have mixed emotions, thoughts, and instincts—good and bad. When Twos give themselves latitude to be less attached to virtues alone and allow room for a full spectrum of traits, from selfishness to selflessness, they will feel less imprisoned by unrealistic self-images. By acknowledging and accepting shortcomings, Type Twos can develop ways to address them and become better without self-condemnation. No one needs to aim for sainthood to be loved. The threshold is much lower in the real world.

When Type Two givers clarify their desires and recognize that taking care of themselves is not the equivalent of being self-centered, it becomes easier to harness the strength of a Type Eight challenger. Out of all Enneagram types, Type Eights are among the bravest personalities when pursuing their objectives. Type Twos need not worry about becoming self-serving megalomaniacs since a healthy Type Eight archetype is anything but. The best leaders are as passionate about fighting for others as they are for themselves. They are discerning with personal boundaries to nurture their needs, knowing when to say yes or no.

Type Two givers take flight when they are no longer wedded to the need to sacrifice for everyone. They calculate their life trajectories with confidence and self-compassion. As these giving personalities chart their paths toward financial independence, they will no longer be hidden figures but rather come into their own.

Chapter 5

Type Three: Madonna

I grew up without a mother, and my father was largely absent until I was thirteen years old, when we started living together under the same roof. A father-son bond did not quite form between us. The lack of parental love and guidance created a void that became foundational to my character development. Only in recent years have I seen how the exclusion of maternal love and ambivalence toward my paternal figure shaped my Type Five personality.

Family relations were distant and cordial at best during my early teenage years. Open conflict was common, as I did not know how to express my emotional needs in healthy ways or understand what my unconventional upbringing had done to my psyche. I struggled to explain where my mother was to anyone who asked. Consequently, I became more guarded and withdrawn. Amid these confusing times, someone appeared in my life to provide some much-needed direction.

That someone was Madonna.

As cheesy as it may sound, she filled the role of my mother during my formative years. I suspect Madonna played a similar part for many gay men of my generation. She is an LGBTQIA+ icon for a reason.

The year was 1993. I bought my first Madonna album, which came with a "parental advisory" sticker. That warning did not deter me. In fact, it was probably why I bought it since no one was giving me advice anyway—the ironic allure of such warnings to adolescents. Playing the album, I was shocked yet captivated by her explicitness. *Who is this person?* I wondered. For the first time in my life, I took an interest in reading, diving into books and magazines on Madonna. It was not just her songs that resonated with me. Deep down, I was (and still am) drawn to her intellect, willpower, "blonde ambition," and refreshing boldness in speaking her mind.

With Madonna providing inspiration, I began to strive harder rather than merely enjoying unsupervised freedom or dwelling in my inner world. She taught me to conquer fears, take up space, and aim higher in life despite being dealt a shorter hand. Most of all, Madonna encouraged me to accept myself as gay in a country that codified male homosexuality as a crime until late 2022.

Looking back, she transformed my beliefs during those awkward years and changed the course of my life. Madonna might be polarizing for many, but to my fourteen-year-old self, she was a godsend when I needed a mentor the most. I developed an image of Madonna, and that was how I experienced her. It was an idealized version, but it worked.

Without a doubt, Madonna is a quintessential Type Three performer: savvy, influential, and always in vogue. She oozes confidence, enough to parade naked in public and on camera; I could not even look at my body in the mirror when I was a teenager. Consistent with the best of Type Threes, Madonna is a formidable taskmaster, often speaking about her disciplined and relentless work ethic. Part of that drive is rooted in her childhood, defined by her mother's passing when she was just five years old. Perhaps that made me look up to Madonna even more; she fulfilled an unconscious desire for reassurance that I might also have a chance of thriving.

Of the nine Enneagram personalities, Type Three performers will always have a special place in my heart. Oh, my husband is a Type Three as well.

PERSONALITY OF TYPE THREES (PERFORMERS)

Type Threes are practically synonymous with accomplishment; hence, they are also referred to as "performers," "achievers," and "role models" in the Enneagram world.

Energetic and motivated, they are always armed with an agenda to get things done, whether at work or in their personal lives. These ambitious individuals know how to get what they want by being systematic and efficient. Possessing tremendous willpower, outstanding performers demonstrate the meaning of human endurance in the face of great challenges to become paragons of society while retaining superstar magnetism. Lady Gaga, Tom Cruise, and Paul McCartney are examples of role models who have made it to the top with dedication, talent, and charisma.

One may be surprised to learn that Type Threes belong to the same heart triad as Type Twos (givers) and Type Fours (individualists) since the latter two archetypes exhibit softer and more emotional traits in their behaviors. Typical Type Twos are affectionate and eager to show the warmth they feel for others, while Type Fours are the introspective ones who like to express a full range of emotions. In contrast, many Type Threes give the impression of being all business and task-oriented.

Despite appearances, all heart types register feelings more than thoughts and instincts. The three Enneagram personalities just cope with them in dissimilar ways, especially to ward off shame. Type Two givers focus on relationships and try to be as valuable to others as possible to feel appreciated. Type Four individualists dig deep into their inner worlds to find differentiating qualities. On the other hand, Type Three performers focus on personifying the cultural definition of success to feel worthy. They learn to swap their hearts for deliberate planning and action from a young age. Believing emotions to be irrelevant or even counterproductive, performers become practiced at compartmentalization. However, the same detachment can cause disconnection from (and denial of) emotional needs, resulting in them identifying only with socially acceptable objectives to feel valued for what they do rather than simply being who they are on the inside.

In the corporate world, these high achievers can be vigorous in their upward climb, driven by a competitive streak to best position themselves. Some focus on improving their professional competencies, while others are better at navigating office politics. Often, they succeed in securing the recognition they crave, including titles, corner offices, accolades, and acclaim. Many Type Threes are therefore workaholics and may prioritize career advancement over family or health.

In social settings, Type Threes are almost always well put together. No matter how they feel inside, Type Threes fine-tune their emotional landscapes to project confidence on the outside. Image is paramount. What they wear may be more than just fashion; it is a cloak and armor. These charming chameleons can read any room they walk into and figure out what they need to say or do to fit the prevailing milieu. Many people consequently find Type Threes desirable and admirable—precisely how they want to be perceived.

Within the context of intimate relationships, emphasis on outward appearance can have unintended consequences. Sharing vulnerabilities is difficult since Type Threes may not wish to acknowledge weaknesses that run counter to their self-image. They may also have a hard time understanding their feelings after years of practiced repression, let alone articulating them. Owing to these factors, Type Threes tend to ignore the soft, intangible underbellies of emotions to display well-defined characteristics of a model spouse, parent, family member, and close friend. Closeness that requires emotional nakedness can therefore be a challenge.

Well-integrated Type Threes transcend self-consciousness and the need for external validation. Self-acceptance is internalized, and confidence comes from within. They still strive for greater accomplishments, but their pursuits are tempered by a firm grip on who they truly are and not how they want to be seen. Goals are directed inward and aligned with innate desires and values. Even without mainstream approval, healthy Type Threes follow through with their passions. Ironically, when others experience a Type Three's authenticity and strength of character in this way, a spontaneous outpour of admiration often follows, all without any deliberate effort on the part of these performers to earn it.

In contrast, unhealthy Type Threes are driven by vanity. Perception is everything, so they strive to fit any image of success that will garner applause, whether the model in question is a virtuous saint or an all-powerful executive. Whether these performers possess true virtue or authority is secondary since authenticity takes a back seat to persona. While unhealthy Type Threes may still appear picture-perfect, an air of pretension pervades. Think Matt Damon as Tom Ripley in that 1999 movie *The Talented Mr. Ripley*. The protagonist assumes multiple identities in his quest to earn social status and fortune. One line from the movie sums up the personality of an unhealthy Type Three: "I suppose I always thought . . . better to be a fake somebody than a real nobody."

CHECKLIST FOR TYPE THREE

If you respond "Yes" to, or resonate with, most of the questions and the statements below, you are likely to be a Type Three:

- ☐ You dislike confrontation for fear of alienating people or staining your image.

- ☐ Growing up, you strove for your parents' approval and would work hard for accomplishments that you felt could make them proud of you.
- ☐ Checklists, to-do lists, spreadsheets, and productivity apps are tools you like to use to be more efficient and productive, even for your personal activities.
- ☐ When planning vacations, you like to research and book activities ahead of time.
- ☐ Before leaving the house, you are often intentional with your outfit choices as you like to look well put together.
- ☐ You prefer not to discuss your insecurities or uncertainties with others even when you experience them powerfully.
- ☐ Competitiveness is a trait you identify with, and you like to compare yourself to your peers.
- ☐ At work, you are conscious of how you come across to others, especially those whose opinions matter the most to your career advancements.
- ☐ To remain poised on the outside, you have developed a considerable ability to control your emotions.
- ☐ You possess great social instincts and can read people and situations before adapting your behaviors, communication styles, and presentations.

TYPE THREE INVESTORS

Type Threes would undoubtedly make model fund managers if they were to identify with the profession. They are competitive (striving to beat the benchmarks), efficient (imagine them staying on top of disclosures and macro developments), and look the part (dressed to kill) to inspire confidence in clients. Picture the likes of Ray Dalio, Seth Klarman, Sir John Templeton, and Catherine Wood; Type Threes will mold themselves to fit in with the greats and commit to the task.

In their personal capacities, however, managing money behind closed doors may be different. While performers are goal-oriented, focus is usually reserved for career and social objectives. For those who take an interest in exercising more control over personal investing, their personality forces can either make them superb investors when harnessed in unison or haphazard if misaligned with true priorities. In parallel, discretionary spending at odds with fiscal prudence is a potential trap for the image-conscious Type Threes.

CORE MOTIVATIONS: TO BE SIMPLY THE BEST

With their competitive streaks, Type Threes enjoy being the best wherever they go and in whatever they choose to do. If performers are focused on investing, they will be driven to succeed. Perhaps out of a desire to stand out, Type Three investors will make whatever mental, behavioral, and emotional shifts are needed to outperform the benchmark.

On the contrary, if investing is not a concern, Type Threes can be disengaged and pay only scant attention to portfolio matters. Financial planning may be outsourced entirely or consist of just sitting on cash. Without some degree of intentional work, one would have to depend more on external sources of wealth—or a lucrative career—to secure retirement.

PRIMARY INFATUATION: THE RIGHT IMAGE

A potential investing pitfall for a personality that desires admiration is jumping onto bandwagons to be seen as part of the zeitgeist or as prescient investors. If investing in connected fitness or seemingly cutting-edge electric vehicle makers is the trend, Type Threes might dive into the fray without due consideration. If holding Bitcoin makes them feel like part of the cool kids' club, then partaking in it becomes likely. Motivations rooted in the perception of others can distort decision-making, leading to stark misalignment between investments and their inherent merits.

KEY AVOIDANCE: UNDERPERFORMANCE

Type Three investors may veer more toward exchange-traded funds or reputable mutual funds to avoid market underperformance. Responsibility for making bad investment choices is something that the more self-conscious Type Three investors may avoid. There can be neither underperformance nor personal responsibility when tracking broad indices or outsourcing portfolio decisions. This is still a solid outcome for any investor if a coherent investment plan is built around these financial products.

CHIEF PROVOCATION: FAILURE

Many Type Threes cannot abide personal or professional failures. The aversion is rooted in their core fear of feeling unworthy or unlovable if stripped of their successes. Significant stumbles may stir up cognitive dissonance between their genuine selves—multifaceted and flawed—and the polished personas they try so hard to embody. For this reason, Type Threes will work hard to channel all their energies toward ensuring (or redefining) victories.

To avoid failures in investing, some Type Threes may choose to do nothing or the absolute minimum. This psychological setup leads to less risk-taking or none. For example, homeownership might be deferred even if affordability is not an issue since renting presents a lower financial risk profile. Other Type Three investors may set modest goals designed to be easily attained. And if returns do not meet expectations, shortfalls can be attributed to external factors or pushed out of consciousness.

BLIND SPOT #1: INNATE MOTIVATIONS

Paradoxically, performers can be convinced of their mission yet disconnected from their inner selves at the same time. Long-term financial planning is part of a lifelong self-discovery process to uncover future needs that transcend vanity. It is also about finding an investing style that resonates with personal preferences on how involved (whether more passive or active) individuals want to be and how much risk is appropriate at any point in time. Until Type Three investors are clear about their likes, dislikes, risk appetite, priorities, and anticipated needs, they risk operating on autopilot mapped to misconstrued agendas.

BLIND SPOT #2: ALTERNATIVE PERSPECTIVES

Mental openness can be compromised by egocentricity. Because Type Threes value winning more than anything, alternative perspectives may be viewed as implying that the Type Three is wrong and others are right. Their not having thought of other approaches in the first place may even be experienced by the Type Three as admitting intellectual shortcomings.

TYPE THREES: WHEN DEALING WITH INVESTMENT SUCCESSES AND FAILURES

A Type Three's mind, heart, and gut are built for success. Single-mindedness and deep yearnings for validation, combined with little to no hesitation to forge ahead in action, make performers the prime Enneagram personality to thrive, especially in capitalist societies. Personal investing is no exception if it resonates with the mission: Type Threes can be formidable investors and give everyone a master class.

A key Type Three skill most relevant to investing is a superior ability to keep emotions out of decision-making. When significant sums of money are at stake, human senses can play tricks on the mind. People often get carried away and become too rash or fearful to act. Others may dwell on regret, anger, or resentment. Not Type Threes. Years of learning how to compartmentalize can translate into an uncanny ability to remain all business and logical, essential to navigating the personal investing journey. For Type Three investors and their road map, greater success is not so much about doing more but about reinterpretation of goalposts and establishing specific safeguards against getting blindsided.

On the flip side, anyone who pursues investment success for vainglory's sake may become susceptible to tunnel vision. Outsize effects of vanity can create more blind spots, cut short winning investments all too soon, and invite excessive risk-taking without due consideration.

Type Threes may externalize the blame or push investment failures out of consciousness. Admitting mistakes is hard for these high performers, whose self-worth is dependent on an image of success. Investment mistakes are easy to cover up; no one needs to know how much profit and loss exist in one's portfolio, except perhaps the Internal Revenue Service. Actual returns—or lack thereof—can be as private or accountable as one would like. Unhealthy Type Threes may sweep them under the rug to avoid emotional blowback.

There is, however, value in acknowledging and confronting slipups on the investing journey. Jeff Bezos, founder and former CEO of Amazon, once referred to failure and invention as inseparable twins. A capacity for self-reflection allows one to learn from mistakes, even though Type Threes may find them to be an affront to self-worth.

By attributing causes to externalities and abandoning the scene, Type Three investors lose the opportunity to extract lessons that may otherwise prevent the recurrence of the same mistakes.

ROAD MAP FOR TYPE THREE INVESTORS

If Type Three investors set themselves up for the challenge of attaining specific investment goals, they will move mountains to knock them out of the park.

A key question to ask first is how much of the investing process a Type Three wishes to get personally involved in. There are multiple ways to handle personal finances, and while there is little doubt that performers have what it takes to win, some may prefer a more passive approach to focus their energies elsewhere. Not all Type Threes will enjoy active portfolio management. If they identify with the process, then getting into the weeds is apt. Otherwise, they may be better suited to outsourcing certain aspects of their road map.

That said, all Type Threes should exercise a degree of discretion in their personal investing journeys, whether in the form of goal setting or heightening self-awareness of fiscal realities and potential pitfalls.

TABULATE NET WORTH

As John Doerr suggests in his book *Measure What Matters*, a few simple tabulations should ground Type Three investors further in reality and set them on a more robust path toward conscious financial planning. Stocks, fixed income, real estate, and any asset with high liquidation value count toward the asset side of the personal balance sheet. Clothes, furniture, and possessions, in general, should be excluded. Aggregation of all liabilities—including student loans, credit card debt, mortgages, and even buy-now-pay-later amounts owed—drop into the other side. The difference between assets and liabilities is net worth, which should give Type Three investors better bearings on their financial conditions. Type Threes should repeat this process at least once a year.

SET EXPLICIT FINANCIAL GOALS

It takes deliberation for investors to clarify long-term financial needs and the pivots necessary to reach further objectives. As major life changes transpire, fiscal requirements will also transform, necessitating changes to portfolio risk profile, cash flow allocation to investment accounts, and budget controls.

Type Three investors should set some strategic directions periodically and decide what to do to stay on track. Setting annual or multiyear targets has the effect of sharpening one's mind to attain them. Investment metrics may include homeownership by a certain age or the amount of capital to deploy into diversified portfolios.

The objective here is to align a performer's intrinsic love for goal setting with financial planning, and the process should also involve external parties like financial planners for greater accountability and alternative perspectives.

SECURE HOMEOWNERSHIP

Securing one's first home can be a great source of pride that goes beyond any discretionary purchase. It confers a deep sense of self-possession, which can feel especially anchoring to Type Threes, who tend to look outward for validation. Homeownership also represents a significant and tangible milestone in life, further empowering Type Three investors.

Having to pay a monthly mortgage like clockwork is also one of the best ways to instill fiscal discipline. It channels funds toward building equity (by lowering mortgage principal) and away from tempting but nonessential spending. This is especially important during the early stages of one's career when disposable income rises and YOLO ("You only live once") forces beckon. Provided that proper due diligence has been done on the choice of real estate, Type Three investors should make the purchase as soon as there are sufficient funds for a down payment.

SET UP A REGULAR INVESTMENT ACCOUNT

With full agendas from professional and social endeavors, Type Threes will benefit from the convenience of automated contributions to retirement plans and index funds (covering both stocks and fixed income) that are easy to execute. Regular investment plans take advantage of dollar-cost averaging and remove the burden of market timing, allowing Type Threes to focus on other pursuits without missing a beat on growing portfolio depth. Diversification should drive the choice of funds in their portfolios, spread across multiple geographies, industries, asset classes, and risk profiles.

OBSERVE FEARS OF MISSING OUT (FOMO)

Type Three investors may be easily swayed by investing trends, not so much because of the potential payoff but from a desire to be part of a popular narrative. Social networking sites fuel perceptions of missing out on material goods and indulgent experiences, and organizations and individuals use them to promote their latest investments, which can lean more toward the sensational and speculative. Type Threes may then feel tempted to jump on board to be considered ahead of the curve without spending enough time on due diligence.

If Type Threes make specific investments, aggregate amounts should be subject to a low cap. Each name must not constitute more than 2.5 percent of the total portfolio (based on capital deployed), regardless of how compelling the thesis may be. Diversification is an effective and enduring risk-management principle.

BEWARE OF TAKING CHIPS OFF

An investment challenge that many Type Three investors may face is taking winning chips off the table too soon. There is nothing wrong with cashing profits per se, but if that is motivated by a desire to make large discretionary purchases that border on ostentation, it becomes shortsighted. That luxury item funded by proceeds from a successful investment may end up with a much larger price tag if opportunity cost—what the investment could be worth if retained—is added. Staying invested for the long haul and delaying immediate gratification is important for Type Three investors to reap the total rewards of their investment successes.

DEVELOPMENT PLAN FOR THREES: INTEGRATING TOWARD TYPE SIX (SKEPTIC) AND TYPE NINE (PEACEMAKER)

"I was lying in bed, lacking the will or the energy to get up. I had the greatest job I could ever have imagined at Oracle, one of the fastest-growing software companies in the world. I had been promoted to vice president, the youngest person ever in that position. Soon I had the multi-million-dollar salary, stock, and perks to go with it. I did not feel happy or fulfilled. I was supposedly living the American dream, but I was lost."

Trailblazer by Marc Benioff (2019)

Marc Benioff, then thirty-one years old, was in an emotional quandary. For a decade, he had been on a roll as a consummate salesman at Oracle, the undisputed leader in database technology. At twenty-three, Benioff was named Rookie of the Year; shortly after, he became the youngest person in the company's history to earn the title of vice president. By his mid-twenties, Benioff reportedly made $300,000 annually and drove a Ferrari Mondial Cabriolet. He was even personally mentored for years by Oracle's founder and chief executive officer, Larry Ellison.

In his own words, Benioff was living the American dream.

Yet he was deflated and struggled to pull himself back together in that summer of 1996. Despite his extraordinary career at Oracle, he felt lost. Instead of exerting more self-control to will his way back onto the fast track—as expected of a high-flying Type Three—Benioff made the most uncompetitive and least egotistical career move. He let go and took a sabbatical.

In the following months, Benioff found himself in Southern India, near the backwaters of the Arabian Sea, meeting spiritual leaders for guidance. As he recounts in his book *Trailblazer*, a wise woman told him: "In your quest to succeed and make money, don't forget to do something for others." That break and those specific words would change Benioff's life, planting the seeds for him to blaze his own trail.

After that, Benioff was no longer satisfied with his old job despite enjoying unequivocal success. He wanted to make an impact on the world, starting with a vision to democratize enterprise software solutions over the internet and disrupt the prevailing practice of in-person installation, maintenance, and updates. Instead of hefty upfront investments in hardware and networking that would keep out all except the most endowed of organizations, any customer could access powerful business applications for a small fee on a per-user, per-month basis, delivered immediately in the cloud. In addition, Benioff wanted to design his own corporate culture from scratch, one that was more employee-centric and aligned with his inner yearning to give back to society. He could no longer ignore the incompatibility between his calling and career trajectory at Oracle.

In 1999, Salesforce was born, and it would revolutionize the technology sector with its pioneering software-as-a-service subscription model. It became one of the fastest-growing enterprise software companies in history and consequently forced competitors to rethink their business models. Today, Salesforce is as well known for its cloud-based customer relation management platform as it is for its purposeful employee culture. Benioff also originated and popularized the "1-1-1" philanthropic model, in which corporations set aside 1 percent of equity, 1 percent of product, and 1 percent of employee time for charitable causes.

It is almost illogical to imagine taking one's foot off the gas pedal to accelerate to success, but to Type Threes, this serves a transcendental purpose. Hitting the brakes is akin to a strategic retreat for realignment of being and a reassessment of an autopilot way of doing. In the 2016 Marvel film *Doctor Strange*, these lines, spoken by the Ancient One, sum up the essence of Type Threes and how true change necessitates a shift in perspective:

> *You have such a capacity for goodness. You always excelled, not because you crave success, but because of your fear of failure. It is precisely what kept you from greatness. Arrogance and fear still keep you from learning the simplest and most significant lesson of all. It is not about you.*

The two Enneagram pivots for Type Threes coincide with the same theme of stepping away from self. Type Six (skeptic) and Type Nine (peacemaker) represent bidirectional thinking and instinctual patterns, respectively, that equilibrize the forward charge of a Type Three mind and body. In place of singular pursuits to burnish one's image of being good and successful, the counterbalances introduce healthy skepticism to reassess personal beliefs, as well as harmony from learning to ease into collective strengths.

Rather than being concerned about appearing right or wrong, healthy Type Sixes pause for reflection and seek alternative viewpoints. The blend of intellectual curiosity outside of fail-safe formulas and openness to self-doubt may feel like a dampener to the mission-focused Type Threes, but these qualities are also forcing functions to reexamine underlying assumptions. Slowing down to think like a skeptical Type Six creates additional space to question personal motives beyond the usual rhetoric of getting things done. Moreover, when availing themselves of a chance to be unsure, Type Threes may realize that apprehension, acknowledgment of more than one way to skin a cat, and the possibility of harboring shadow intentions behind overt rationalizations need not threaten their sense of self or safety. After all, we humans are all complex, multidimensional, and deeply flawed beings who can only try to do better once we know better.

While a Type Nine ethos of going with the flow may run counterintuitive to the Type Three tendency to exert one's will, meaningful relationships are just as important as individual goals in achieving the veneration Type Threes seek. Performers tend to pay no heed to their emotions to maintain focus, but a brisk dismissal might alienate people. In contrast, healthy Type Nines have an instinctive understanding of self and can intuit what people desire to create win-win solutions because they value harmony with their wider communities. To these peacemakers, collective strength and victories are as empowering as personal triumphs. And it is never a zero-sum game. Type Threes can learn to rely on the combined capabilities of their respective tribes—colleagues, families, spouses, close friends—to problem-solve and flow with a larger rhythm rather than treating life like a one-person show.

Type Three achievers may wish to contemplate their drive for recognition, which can cause emotional distress when the desired external image they crave is inconsistent with their true selves. Much of it may be rooted in feelings of inadequacy. Type Threes can look back at their childhood for clues: Were they compelled to accomplish certain results—grades, medals, cheerleader or athlete stature, applause—to please their caretakers and gain their attention, as opposed to feeling unconditionally loved? Many performers learned to bury their natural desires so as to meet explicit and implicit expectations at a young age, inadvertently blunting their sensitivities to emotional needs. When they reach adulthood, Type Threes go straight to identifying culturally acceptable goals that will secure similar approval and admiring looks, without being able to discern whether those directions befit their hearts' desires.

When it comes to personal investing, it is as much about the journey as it is about monetary outcomes. Healthy Type Three investors strike a balance among saving, investing, and spending. Without the need to attain certain results to outmatch someone or make a statement purchase, their relationship with money is calibrated according to their inherent selves. Healthy Type Threes who do not like managing active portfolios might only commit to index or mutual funds, homeownership, and perhaps investment properties. They will recruit external parties to handle their finances while remaining fully aware of their present financial situation and future goals. As for Type Threes who are passionate about taking charge of their finances, they will put in hard work behind the scenes because they enjoy the learning process. They are not afraid to make mistakes, and they perform a proper postmortem, hence benefiting from each failure rather than sweeping it under the carpet of immaculate appearances. They seek alternative opinions and views to supplement their shortcomings before making investment decisions—without being hurried or compelled by FOMO.

At Oracle, Marc Benioff was a star employee. Had he stayed, he likely would have become one of the top executives as Ellison's protégé. Yet the high opportunity cost and risk of potential failure in starting a brand-new venture did not stop Benioff from following his passion. He took an enormous financial risk and seeded Salesforce with the $6 million he had saved over a decade. But by changing course to realign with his values, listening to his heart, and shifting his focus away from himself, he changed the world. Salesforce put Benioff on the pedestal of America's most inspirational entrepreneurs, right next to his mentor, Ellison.

Type Threes can realize their own dreams, not just the American dream, when they hit the pause button and reconnect with the emotional realm. Marc Benioff did precisely that after losing his mojo and got it back in spades as the iconic founder of Salesforce.

Chapter 6

Type Four: Cruella De Vil (of *Cruella*)

"From the very beginning, I've always made a statement. I am woman. Hear me roar."

Cruella (2021)

In a voiceover at the start of the 2021 Disney film *Cruella,* the title character declares she is not for everyone and sees the world differently. Scenes of her as a little girl designing an avant-garde outfit for her teddy bear instead of the suggested plain sweater template reveal she is someone who defies conformity. It is evident just minutes into the film that young Cruella is driven to assert her identity, making her an archetypal Type Four (individualist).

Cruella De Vil was created in 1956 by British author Dodie Smith. Cast as a one-dimensional villain, she was a caricature in previous movies: a tyrannical fashion designer obsessed with furs and especially determined to turn Dalmatian puppies into her coat collection. She was an Anna Wintour gone mad. Or a female version of Mugatu from *Zoolander* (2001). The first two live-action adaptations—*101 Dalmatians* (1996) and *102 Dalmatians* (2000)—did not deviate far from the cartoon-like formula.

Then, the 2021 version starring Emma Stone came along and took character development to another level. This is Cruella's origin story, something Walt Disney had not covered before. The film presents a more humane side and chronicles her early days well before she grows into a full-fledged villain. Watching the movie, one cannot help but feel a degree of empathy for a person whose birth mother immediately tries to get rid of her. That would mess up anyone's mind. Skinning animals for fur seems like a mild psychological consequence in the aftermath of such trauma. I am surprised Cruella did not become more like Buffalo Bill in *The Silence of the Lambs* (1991)!

The first act introduces Cruella as a twelve-year-old child, Estella. Brimming with creativity and sporting distinctive hair parted between natural black and white, she is a force of nature, challenging the world. Estella is unafraid to be herself in school, refusing to be repressed by staid uniforms (she wears a fashionable jacket over hers), standing up to bullies (she takes on boys in schoolyard fights), and rejecting any attempt to cover up her black-and-white hair for the sake of blending in. As she explains in the film, she pretty much roars her way all through primary school until she gets expelled.

In a tragic turn of events, Estella ends up alone in London and is forced to survive as a grifter, along with her street urchin friends, Jasper and Horace. At this point in the film, Estella is living far below her potential, and her first act of survival is to dye her hair dark, symbolizing a rejection of her true self.

Until she meets Baroness von Hellman.

The film takes a few major twists and turns from there, but we see her creativity in full force as a guerrilla fashion designer hell-bent on taking down the baroness. Along with resurgent creativity, Cruella's growing hostility is unleashed without discrimination, even on Jasper and Horace, the only two people who care for her. This is where her character again struggles with identity. While she may be embracing her authentic self after a decade of suppression, Cruella also starts to reject her modern family, acting as if she does not need or want them. It is not until a brush with death (and subsequent revelations) that she reins in her belligerence toward Jasper and Horace.

As extraordinary as she may be, Cruella is also human, and she recognizes her common but essential need for support from close relationships. She reestablishes her bond with Jasper and Horace by jailbreaking them in the most dramatic way. Reconciling with her past, Cruella takes a more measured and intelligent approach to her personal vendetta against the baroness in the last act.

PERSONALITY OF TYPE FOURS (INDIVIDUALISTS)

Not all Type Fours wear their personalities like Cruella, with black-and-white hair and punk-rock couture. They do, however, have one thing in common: the willful display of individuality. Their expressions can be in the form of enjoying cool indie music, creating original artwork, wearing eclectic combinations of clothing and accessories, or showing unusual depths of emotions. To be like everyone else does not motivate them. Not only do Type Fours want to be true to themselves, but they also yearn to be different from others. They may, therefore, resist holding a regular job like their peers or living a lifestyle subscribed to by the majority.

That drive to separate oneself from the masses can cut both ways. When combined with grounded intelligence and hard work, a healthy Type Four joins the ranks of creative geniuses like Taylor Swift and David Bowie. On the other hand, a single-minded need to be different can lead to poor choices that are not rooted in reality. An insular belief that one is unique and therefore exempt from having to endure the due process in any endeavor is delusional.

Type Fours are the most in touch with their feelings out of all Enneagram types. With much more inward focus than either of the two other heart types—Threes (performers) and Twos (givers)—Type Fours (individualists) are marked by their heightened self-awareness. Many of them are thus introspective, which can be a mixed blessing.

On the one hand, they have more clarity regarding their inner worlds and hence are more aware of latent feelings and thoughts. On the other hand, with such an intense interiority, it becomes easy to get lost and slide into self-consciousness. Or worse, self-absorption.

The best Type Fours transcend their rich inner worlds—good and bad—into reinvention without self-consciousness or self-absorption. Rather than just feeling misunderstood and turning inward, healthy Type Fours channel their emotions outward into creative expression. They are grounded and connected to the outside world yet remain in touch with their inner selves. Neither impulsive nor rebellious for the sake of being different, they believe they are unique beings through productive actions, not by birthright. They still see themselves as part of this world and as humans. Hence, they stay relatable and relevant, not otherworldly.

Frida Kahlo, a Mexican painter known for her autobiographical and often shocking work, once said, "My painting carries with it the message of pain." One of her most famous paintings is the surreal *My Birth*, which depicts Frida Kahlo giving birth to herself. It is a haunting and unsettling image. Painted in 1932, *My Birth* incorporates emotional elements from Frida Kahlo's prior miscarriage and the loss of her mother. Today, it is regarded as one of her masterpieces.

Meanwhile, unhealthy Type Fours are often consumed by their melancholy, dwelling on their pain and despair. Instead of resolving their intensity constructively, unhealthy Type Fours withdraw from others to wallow. In the film *Cruella*, Cruella says she is "born brilliant, born bad, and a little bit mad." When Cruella takes this narrative too far, especially the bits about being bad and mad, she pushes her allies away and suffers dire consequences that almost cost her life. Introversion in the extreme becomes self-alienation. People within their inner circles may find such brooding moodiness draining and start to distance themselves. Unhealthy Type Fours also tend to be hypersensitive to the emotions of people around them, further compounding their already overwhelming inner worlds.

Pains, when indulged, may push them into self-torment and self-destruction. Think tortured artists like Vincent van Gogh, Édith Piaf, and Janis Joplin.

CHECKLIST FOR TYPE FOUR

If you respond "Yes" to, or resonate with, most of the questions and the statements below, you are likely to be a Type Four:

- ☐ You feel it is important to represent the real you to the world, including choosing the right attire, selecting exact home furnishings that reflect your self-image, and posting the pictures on social media that are most meaningful.
- ☐ In your choice of profession, you believe in finding the ideal job that fits your identity and creativity more so than what is the most coveted or in-demand career path.
- ☐ You would rather be unique and unpopular than be popular but resemble everyone else.
- ☐ Casual teases or jokes can make you feel vulnerable and hurt for extended periods.
- ☐ Between being practical and being authentic, the latter resonates more.
- ☐ You have always had an eye for aesthetics and are drawn to various creative art forms.
- ☐ Compared to your peers, you feel you are more introspective.
- ☐ You are comfortable experiencing a full spectrum of intense emotions, from profound sadness to absolute joy.

- ☐ Rather than pure quantitative analysis and exploration of multiple scenarios, you rely on feelings and intuition just as much (if not more) in your approach to problem-solving.
- ☐ You can be quite moody and put off mundane but essential tasks (such as reordering groceries, filing tax returns, and attending to a home repair) until you are in the right mood.

TYPE FOUR INVESTORS

Given the importance of identity to Type Fours, everything they do—how they look, what they consume, and where they work—must resonate. If something does not feel right, it is unlikely to stick.

The same applies to financial matters. Without feeling it, a Type Four individual will not be inclined to invest, regardless of inherent merits or what others say. Some Fours may even embrace disdain for capitalism to spite collective beliefs and align themselves with idealistic anti-capitalists. On the flip side, Type Four investors who dream about becoming the next Benjamin Graham or Carl Icahn will pursue personal investing with wholehearted relish.

Fiscal responsibility cannot be achieved based on emotions alone. It requires a more thoughtful and structured approach. An "I feel, therefore I am" style in investment decisions could lead to arbitrary and capricious capital deployments. Fantasy—something that Type Fours are prone to—can also lure them into Ponzi-esque schemes that promise them the world.

This does not mean investment decisions should be made with clinical precision without regard to what an investment means about a Type Four's sense of self. For example, a Type Four investor who advocates environmental causes should not be investing in oil majors.

CORE MOTIVATION: TO DIFFERENTIATE

To be different takes courage because it can be risky. In the animal kingdom, prey animals stay together in packs to protect against being singled out by predators. Regarding personal investing, the equivalent of such self-protective moves may include portfolio allocations to index funds, home equity, gold, cash savings, and large capitalization companies, which are safer since these are conventional. Will this resonate with Type Four investors who yearn to be different? Unlikely. They possess ample courage to stand out, partly because they feel they are exceptions to the rule. How idiosyncratic bets pan out depends on the guardrails they employ and—like it or not—luck.

In the early 2000s, taking an investment risk on Netflix would likely have appealed to Type Four investors because the company was a disruptor to the traditional movie rental business with its DVD-by-mail subscription model. Reed Hastings and Marc Randolph, cofounders of Netflix, were the kind of purpose-driven mavericks who would stir up many Type Four rebels to stick it to the establishment, which was Blockbuster (with its infamous late-fee charges) at that time. Investing in Netflix then (it went public in 2002) would have yielded superb results.

Unfortunately, more cases of disruptors end up in disasters than in the pantheon of glory. Webvan and Pets.com went up in smoke. A host of current electric vehicle challengers that emerged after Tesla's success will also fail to scale and so enter the corporate graveyard.

PRIMARY INFATUATION: DWELLING IN THEIR EMOTIONAL BASEMENTS

As rebellious as Type Four individualists can be in the bid to be different, their emotional realms can be more susceptible to moodiness and dark feelings than positive ones. This becomes an issue when dealing with setbacks on their investing journeys. If something does not pan out, Type Four investors can become overwhelmed by profound sadness and dwell on their inner distress longer than they should. Shame and excessive rumination on negative thoughts add to their melancholy, detracting from their self-esteem and preventing constructive steps from being taken.

KEY AVOIDANCE: SNAPPING OUT OF IT

Type Four investors tend to detach from reality. A combination of could-haves, should-haves, would-haves, and if-onlys can suck them into a vortex of inaction. If they had missed out on securing homeownership at bottom pricing during the 2008 global financial crisis, unhealthy Type Fours might have luxuriated in regret and dissatisfaction rather than launching into an earnest search for another suitable property. Or they might have fantasized about an imagined home without taking concrete steps to realize it.

Rumination leads nowhere. All the energy spent on anger, lamentation, and fantasies takes Type Four investors away from carrying out actual investment plans. Despite how good melancholy may taste, they must get out of themselves and their feelings to start moving forward. Borrowing from Cher's iconic line in the 1987 film *Moonstruck*, Type Four investors need to "snap out of it!"

CHIEF PROVOCATION: WHEN SOMEONE INVESTS BETTER

A Type Four's need to be different entails constant comparison with others, and these individualists may get carried away envying anyone who does better. The green monster goes hand in hand with feelings of inadequacy about one's own financial journey, and when that monster rears its head, it can provoke impulsive reactions. Type Four investors who are usually conservative may start jumping into riskier bets, regardless of portfolio suitability, knowledge, or personality fit.

BLIND SPOT #1: PLAIN VANILLA INVESTMENTS

Plain vanilla investing is essential to building the foundations in one's portfolio and kick-starting a lifelong learning journey regarding personal finances. While stock picking, venture capital, private equity, derivatives, and the like may promise supernova alpha, they are also highly complex. When mismanaged, which is often only evident in hindsight, this can wipe one out financially.

Diversification via index funds, homeownership, repayment of expensive student loans, fixed-income instruments, and even gold, though pedestrian, should not be skipped over in favor of big bets. Regardless, Type Fours may disdain anything ordinary and yearn for something exotic to manifest their dream portfolios. Rather than starting slow and steady to learn the ropes of basic investing principles, Type Four investors may pander to their dreams of hitting jackpots without acknowledging the need to gain expertise first. This makes them susceptible to new flavors in the investment world, like cutting-edge but unproven technologies, anything metaverse, early-stage investing, and whatever Bored Ape Yacht Club nonfungible tokens celebrities are hawking on television.

BLIND SPOT #2: INVESTMENT GODS ARE NOT SUPERHUMAN

One need not have invested in Apple like Warren Buffett did in 2016 to achieve success in investing. Or possess incredible foresight like those storied investors who purchased Amazon stock in 1997 when it became public as an online bookseller. Bemoaning what we missed by comparing ourselves to the so-called clairvoyants of the investment world may exacerbate feelings of lack, which are not conducive to self-empowerment.

We can all do well in personal investing, but Type Four investors might forget their innate abilities while gazing enviously at the lionized icons of investments. These idols are humans, not gods, and have made mistakes that are simply not as publicized as their successes. Rather than idealizing others and their victories, Type Fours should appreciate the strengths they bring to their own investing journeys and formulate a plan to gather more. People do not achieve overnight success with personal investing; capital, skills, knowledge, and emotional strength in managing through cycles are built over time. While comparison is a natural human condition and can be motivating, it must not discourage one's self-belief when embarking on an investing journey.

TYPE FOURS:
WHEN DEALING WITH INVESTMENT SUCCESSES AND FAILURES

Once money is deployed into investments, the path ahead can go in many directions and is never linear. We do not know what we do not know, but staying connected and adjusting our investment strategies over time to suit changing conditions is essential.

Type Four investors can feel everything in extremes, oscillating back and forth between sheer joy and deep sadness, depending on how investments turn out. Let's say an investment starts multiplying in returns. Emotional highs can be overwhelming, so the Type Four investor who identifies with those feelings may move further from vigilant skepticism. Recall the likes of Macy's, Kodak, and Credit Suisse. They were once big winners in the stock market until they were not. To remain grounded is challenging for Type Four investors, especially when things appear rosy.

The more dire scenario is when things do not pan out. This is where Type Four investors are at their most vulnerable. Their natural tendency toward self-loathing makes blunders harder to overcome. The more

Type Four investors sink into a state of duress when staring at their missteps, the more their feelings become a dominant reality for them, inhibiting rectifying actions that ought to be taken. All that woulda-shoulda-coulda can be counterproductive, making Type Four investors sink further into self-doubt, confusion, and feelings of failure and give up altogether. On the other hand, healthy Type Four investors acknowledge painful blunders and soldier on the wiser, making concrete adjustments to their financial journeys to extract value from past mistakes.

ROAD MAP FOR TYPE FOUR INVESTORS

Type Fours can be among the most creative investors with their acuity regarding beauty and aesthetics. They are attracted to beauty because it bathes their inner landscapes with warmth and reinforces their sense of uniqueness. Paintings produced by up-and-coming artists, publicly listed fashion houses like Capri (parent of Michael Kors, Jimmy Choo, and Versace) and Tapestry (Coach, Kate Spade, and Stuart Weitzman), and producers of upmarket home furnishings like Restoration Hardware are likely to appeal to Type Four investors. Less obvious but equally alluring companies can include Apple and Tesla, with their sleek hardware, seamless software integration, and corporate culture designed to create exceptional customer experiences.

Type Four investors may spot early trends in consumer markets quicker than any other Enneagram type due to their ability to read people's emotions. A connoisseur of high fashion, for example, might have noticed how Gucci connected with a new generation of younger consumers when Alessandro Michele was appointed creative director in 2015 and made prescient investments in Kering, Gucci's parent company.

Healthy Type Four investors are excellent judges of individuals, as insightful regarding the outside world as they are with respect to themselves. This sixth sense separates the Steve Jobs of the world from Elizabeth Holmes of Theranos, Kenneth Lay of Enron, and Trevor Milton of Nikola. On the other hand, unhealthy Type Four investors are prone to acting on their emotional impulses. Consider a scenario in which movie-loving Type Four investors decide to invest significant sums in AMC Entertainment—a global chain of theaters—just because they enjoy watching films on the big screen. Or they want to stick it to the institutional short sellers. Such impulsivity might not work out well in the long run as streaming continues to eat into theatrical distribution, despite what Reddit might say about this meme stock.

Guardrails are therefore necessary to mitigate emotionally driven investment decisions that may derail Type Fours from their investing journeys. They need some structure to regulate and provide a counterbalance.

LEAN INTO PLAIN VANILLA INVESTMENTS

Yes, investing like everyone else is not unique, but it effectively counterbalances the kind of avant-garde ideas that Type Fours love but may implode spectacularly. One of the earlier steps to take—alongside paying down expensive student loans and saving emergency cash—is to set up regular investment plans into index funds. I would suggest just the S&P 500 to keep it simple and gain economic exposure to a wide range of businesses. The purpose is multifold. An automatic system that deploys fixed amounts of cash into safer investments establishes early fiscal discipline not subject to mood swings. When deployments are sustained over multiple market cycles, they grow in resilience due to dollar-cost averaging, and with time, having a diversified and stable portfolio will boost a Type Four investor's sense of financial security.

PRIORITIZE HOMEOWNERSHIP

Beyond the usual investment merits of homeownership, the emotional rewards from having one's own nesting place (and private sanctuary in times of melancholy) are irrefutable to a Type Four investor. Type Fours will feel more connected to their immediate environment if they own it. They get free rein over how they want to decorate their homes, akin to having a 3D canvas on which to exercise unrestrained creativity, which can be therapeutic. Homeownership is therefore an investment goal that can yield both financial and emotional payback. However, Type Fours must be careful not to get carried away by feelings and risk overpaying. Rushing to buy in a housing bubble could erase substantial equity value and engulf one in excessive debt. Enlist the right advisers when making such a significant investment.

INVEST IN CREATIONS

If a Type Four has an interest and expertise in art, rare artifacts, or jewelry, it can be worthwhile to diversify one's investment portfolio into such alternative investment classes. The right art pieces can fetch returns that private equity investors and venture capitalists would be jealous of. The art trade, though, is unregulated and full of pitfalls: illiquidity, fraud, price-fixing, opaque commissions, sketchy dealers, and quasi-advisers, just to name a few. While Type Fours may have an eye for future masterpieces and enjoy the process of hunting for artwork, it is best to limit art collection to a small portion of one's portfolio.

LIMIT EXPOSURE TO INDIVIDUAL STOCKS

Emotionally charged Type Fours are especially susceptible to impulse buying and selling, making the stock market a potential trap for them. The additional burden of watching a stock price rise and fall could add to emotional volatility, especially if that portfolio position is significant. Type Fours may still wish to be part owners of companies producing products and services that appeal to them. This approach is espoused by Peter Lynch, who advocates investing in companies that one is familiar with. There are qualifiers to observe, such as transaction prices relative to estimated valuations and the fiscal health of investee companies. Type Four investors must have a solid appreciation of such criteria when picking individual stocks, and a hard limit (say 10 to 20 percent) on the amount of portfolio capital dedicated to stock picking should also be observed. Otherwise, purchasing sector-specific exchange-traded funds can be an excellent middle ground.

AVOID SPECULATIVE INVESTMENTS

It is easy to jump on any new investment bandwagon, given how frictionless it is to open accounts with platforms like Robinhood and Coinbase and trade everything from exotic options to cryptocurrencies. If there is sufficient demand for an emerging asset class, regardless of inherent investment merits, someone out there will create an exchange to make money off transactions. It is no different from a gold rush: Instead of shovels and picks, online tools that enable shuffling of ownership are developed to catalyze feeding frenzies on a global scale. Type Fours may enjoy the initial emotional rush, but without proper due diligence and restraint, the potential impact of capital losses could do real damage to their emotional well-being.

HIRE AND CONNECT WITH FINANCIAL PLANNERS AND ADVISERS

Type Fours may feel misunderstood and therefore believe that only they can carry out plans for their unique financial requirements. The truth is, we all feel misconstrued sometimes and refuse help.

But emotional perception is not reality when it comes to managing money, and we could all use external advice to offset our blind spots and weaknesses. The best counterweight to the emotionally prone Type Four is a suitable Type One perfectionist. Hiring advisers who are detail-oriented, organized, and strict with rules will be a solid guardrail for Type Four investors to prevent (or at least minimize) irrational decisions.

DEVELOPMENT PLAN FOR FOURS:
INTEGRATING TOWARD TYPE ONE (PERFECTIONIST)
AND TYPE TWO (GIVER)

Let's say a friend confides in you about her romantic life with the following: "I always wake up screaming from dreaming that one day he will leave me because he gets tired of my scheming. One day, I'll watch as he leaves, and life will lose all its meaning. I know I am the problem between us. It is me, and everybody agrees. Must be exhausting having to root for me."

You might think of her as a self-referential drama queen and wonder how much time she devotes to having a pity party. Except that the above is lifted almost verbatim from the song "Anti-Hero" written by Taylor Swift, one of the most successful musicians of all time and famed for her autobiographical lyrics. How can Swift—a definite Type Four romantic—be so dramatic and still be this prolific? At thirty-two, she had already released ten studio albums. Her feelings, however pronounced, do not inhibit her productivity or turn her into a recluse.

The ability to experience the full range of human emotions and develop self-awareness is essential to personal development. Type Fours are especially good at digging deep into themselves when mining for meaning and reflections. Nevertheless, that inwardness must not replace definitive actions to move forward and reach new goals. Swift has transformed her melodrama into authentic and relatable music. Discipline in action moves her to connect with people via her abundant output. She is a model Type Four individual who not only is unique but also has harnessed acute awareness of her inner struggles—even painful ones—into creative works for the world to enjoy. Her songs inspire fans who feel the same about their heartbreaks.

With each album, Swift continues reinventing herself, evidenced by her ever-shifting songwriting styles, eclectic collaborations, and fluid genres. Through it all, she remains connected with her feelings and external reality. Her marketing savvy and unprecedented power moves in the face of detractors have rewritten the rules of engagement in the music industry.

What can Type Fours learn from Taylor Swift, and what does this have to do with personal investment? For a start, we can observe how feelings must work in lockstep with action and identity. If all Swift did was wallow in negative self-image, which is spotlighted in many of her songs without self-consciousness, she would be a sad individual, not the prolific singer-songwriter-performer-mogul she is today. Type Fours must recognize that their feelings are not the sole determinants of their identities and are meant to be worked through. Renewal of self is rooted in a combination of introspection and action. There must be a balance between staying connected with feelings to inform self-awareness and living an active life of connecting with the outside world.

Regarding personal investing, Type Four investors need to keep moving forward, regardless of successes, failures, stumbles, or outright disasters. Feelings can magnify when money is involved, so Type Four investors must lean harder into the discipline of a Type One (perfectionist) to act more on rational rules and principles of personal finances. Type Four investors can draw inspiration from the ever-resolute Type Ones to act with grit and conviction, freeing themselves from the traps of their relentless moods. Sticking to a long-term plan to commit capital consistently to growing one's portfolio is crucial in attaining results.

As much as Type Fours enjoy imagining jackpot investments, 100-baggers are rare. Making a bet that will pay off in spades is possible, but a steady, focused approach is far more reliable. Taylor Swift started her career writing standard country music to hone her craft. As she gained momentum and experience, she started sampling different sounds and images to expand her playbook. As unique as she is, she still puts out music that appeals to a broad audience, striking a delicate balance between authenticity and popularity. Similarly, Type Four investors must start on firmer ground in their financial journeys. Only after a strong foundation in knowledge, portfolio composition, and emotional maturity is built should they begin injecting some experimental investments into their repertoire—while never staking their entire safety nets on capricious bets.

A core feature of a Type Four belief system is that the self is broken in some fundamental way. This may stem from childhood experiences that can be hard to erase. Growing up, they may have felt disconnected from their parents or caretakers, so they turn inward to their feelings for comfort. Type Fours develop a habit of introversion to untangle nagging and unceasing emotions, as though something were wrong with them. At the same time, they grow envious of others who seem to possess joy with ease.

When feelings become overwhelming, Type Fours need to step away from themselves, and the best way to do that is to help others. Like with the best Type Two givers, shifting focus can break that spiral of self-consciousness. Type Four investors should consider what financial goals they can formulate to help others, including their spouses, children, parents, or people in need. The best antidote to self-absorption is to love and help others. Though Type Fours may have felt unlovable or unloved during childhood, when they start loving others—in thoughts, feelings, and actions—they will begin to appreciate themselves and the ways those loved ones see them.

Chapter 7

Type Five:
Sherlock Holmes (of *Sherlock Holmes*)

Ever watched the 2009 film *Sherlock Holmes*, directed by Guy Ritchie? Based on the fictional detective created by British author Sir Arthur Conan Doyle, the movie stars Robert Downey Jr., who plays the titular character with an enthralling mix of eccentricity and intelligence. There are over 25,000 stage adaptations, films, television productions, and publications featuring the detective, but I would recommend watching the Guy Ritchie version (also the 2011 sequel, *Sherlock Holmes: A Game of Shadows*) for a more modern take. Robert Downey Jr. does a brilliant job portraying the protagonist, a quintessential Type Five.

In the film, Holmes is often depicted as deep in his thoughts. He conducts unusual and indulgent home experiments on animals—including houseflies—as he secludes himself in his flat for weeks. "There's nothing of interest for me out there on earth," declares Sherlock Holmes to his only friend, Dr. John Watson, who tries to convince him to meet his fiancée, Mary Morsten, over dinner. On any given day, Holmes would rather live in his own world with his own thoughts.

This is classic Type Five behavior. Intellectually, Holmes is almost unequaled in his ability to solve cases. At his best, he is resourceful, perceptive, and in command of himself even in the face of danger.

He connects dots that few can follow and makes inferences like a computer to get from one clue to the next. Those around him can barely keep up. It is no coincidence that Type Fives are commonly known as "investigators" in the Enneagram world.

Socially, however, Holmes is awkward at best.

Consider the dinner scene where he meets Morsten for the first time at a restaurant. At first, we see Holmes seated alone at a large booth. Having arrived fashionably early, he observes everyone around him and absorbs all the minute details, from patrons having an argument to a waiter pocketing a piece of silverware. Though he sits almost motionless, his mind is in hyperdrive, engaged in the mundane. Before his company arrives, Holmes is already preoccupied.

After a quick introduction by Watson, Holmes demonstrates his deductive prowess to Morsten, who encourages him by professing to be a fan of detective novels. Playful at the start, tension builds when Holmes turns his attention to her and wrongly accuses Morsten of being a gold digger. He ends up with wine on his face as his friends turn to leave.

Instead of showing remorse and shame or running after his friends to apologize, Holmes does not react. He seems dissociated and continues to dine alone for the rest of the evening. The next scene cuts to Holmes in an underground boxing match against a muscular opponent. It is as if physical pain and exhaustion are more manageable for him than confronting the sadness of having possibly alienated Watson for good with his highly offensive accusation. Fighting is a coping mechanism for Holmes to decompress and detach from his emotions. For all his investigative talents, he is unable (or unwilling) to dig into his feelings.

Solitude is a recurring theme for Holmes in the film. His ability to perform as a first-rate private detective allows him the financial means to withdraw into his own world between assignments. At the same time, his tendency to seek solace in isolation is accentuated to tragic effect when his love interest, Irene Adler, dies in the sequel.

PERSONALITY OF TYPE FIVES
(INVESTIGATORS)

Type Fives love digging deep into anything that captures their imagination. From a scientist engrossed in experiments inside a laboratory to someone obsessed with conspiracy theories, these investigators represent the cerebral realm—alongside Type Sixes (skeptics) and Type Sevens (enthusiasts)—more than the others. Unlike Type Sixes, who shuffle between internal thoughts and external opinions, or Type Sevens, seeking mental stimulation from outside experiences, investigators are rooted in their minds.

Knowledge is power to Type Fives. It is their primary defense against fear of the external world and helplessness. There is no end to the learning journey, though subject matters can range from constructive pursuits like breakthrough innovations benefiting humanity to peculiar quirks. These thinkers find everything they need in their minds and are seldom bored.

Taken to the extreme, knowledge accumulation can become a hindrance. A simple illustration is a Type Five who tries to learn dancing by observing others boogie or watching YouTube videos at home—everything but hitting the dance floor themselves. Often, these observers feel a sense of perpetual unpreparedness, preferring to think more before acting. Delaying or depriving themselves of active participation inhibits true learning.

By and large, Type Fives tend to blaze their trails alone. Part of that motivation stems from a fear of being overwhelmed by—or overreliance on—external parties. Rather than reaching out for help or fostering symbiotic relationships, Type Fives minimize personal attachments by counting only on themselves. This does not suggest that all Type Fives are loners, but self-sufficiency is the modus operandi, and hence, relationships are not the focus.

Another Type Five characteristic is a deep-seated belief in one's energy and resources being finite. This is rooted in a scarcity mindset, which prompts them to hoard their capacities for self-preservation. Picture having a smartphone with only 20 percent battery left and no power sources in sight for the rest of the day. One would limit usage to only the essential applications—Tinder might count, depending on personal circumstances—out of caution. Such is how investigators regard their time, energy, and needs. Retreating into themselves and economizing their requisites are battery-saving modes.

Healthy Type Fives can strike a balance between internalization and externalization. Conviction is balanced with curiosity about external viewpoints. Seclusion is not an option because they have no unfounded fear of being exhausted by external demands. This implies a shift to an abundance mindset: Internal energy and resources are deemed replenishable; encountering and engaging with the world can reinvigorate the mind. The best thinkers have the fortitude to participate in productive debates.

Understanding that success is built on execution, a healthy investigator dives in without getting caught up in excessive preparation. True confidence results from doing, not just conceptualizing. The most accomplished Type Fives operate without fear and bring pioneering ideas to fruition through persistent action, extensive collaborations, and enlivening engagements. Think of Bill Gates, Stephen Hawking, and Jane Goodall as exemplary personalities of this cerebral kind.

CHECKLIST FOR TYPE FIVE

If you respond "Yes" to, or resonate with, most of the questions and the statements below, you are likely to be a Type Five:

- ☐ You possess in-depth knowledge of particular subjects, which can be a specific field of academic study or Drake's entire album discography in reverse chronological order.
- ☐ You tend to be stingy with yourself, believing you do not need as many adventurous experiences or material possessions as your peers seem to enjoy.
- ☐ Often, you spend time away from friends and family to preserve your energy to engage in your projects.
- ☐ When you concentrate on a task, and someone taps your shoulder, you get startled easily.
- ☐ The word "idiosyncratic" describes you well.
- ☐ When taking academic examinations, you generally prepare well in advance and perform well.
- ☐ Your preference is to rely on yourself—rather than seek help from friends or colleagues—in personal and professional endeavors.
- ☐ Rather than a "Just do it" approach, which you may find reckless, you tend to take your time to observe first and undertake intentional studies before participating in anything new.
- ☐ During childhood, you identified as more separate from (rather than connected to) your parents or caregivers and historically did not have much emotional reliance on them.
- ☐ Social interactions have frequently felt intrusive and draining.

TYPE FIVE INVESTORS

Having a mind of one's own may be an investor's best defense against information overload. Media channels are getting better at turning the uneventful into headlines since clickbait is valuable: The more impressions they generate, the more advertising dollars are earned. Depending on which topics are trending, we could be simultaneously in hyperinflation, deflation, economic recession, or uninterrupted economic expansion. The ability to tune out noise can lend Type Five investors a sense of sanity in this environment.

On the other hand, the same detachment can lead to closed mental loops divorced from changing realities. Sticking one's head in the sand is a common investing phenomenon, especially for Type Five investors who cling to their convictions and disconnect from externalities.

CORE MOTIVATION: TO BE SECURE IN EXPERT KNOWLEDGE

Investigators are on a lifelong mission to learn and make intellectual sense of their external worlds. When contemplating investment opportunities, they dive deep into facts and figures, relishing the research process and gathering an escalating sense of competence. They may get carried away by their fascinations, even if the subjects are no longer relevant to investing. After all those mental gymnastics, a Type Five investor may still feel unprepared or fearful of deploying real capital, preferring to stay secure on the sidelines. In this instance, learning has become a substitute for (instead of an adjunct to) action.

PRIMARY INFATUATION: HOARDING

The term "hoarding" evokes images of someone with mountains

of objects at home—a basic Marie Kondo nightmare. Or perhaps her dream scenario. While a Type Five is often described as someone who curtails needs and dependencies, hence a minimalist, there is also a maximizing urge to hold on to anything that counts toward self-sufficiency.

As knowledgeable as investigators may be, they may not wish to share and exchange ideas with others, believing in the value of information advantage. Hoarding, in this case, impedes healthy discussions on personal investing.

The same avarice applies to financial resources. Suppose spending is regarded as a threat to self-sufficiency. Type Fives may become reluctant to pay for external advice, professional help, or even certain forms of learning if they cost more than what they are willing (versus able) to pay. In penny-pinching style, their battery-saving mode kicks in to rationalize why such expenditures are unnecessary.

Last, since no investment comes without risks, Type Fives may also hold back from investing any money, preferring to hoard cash and equivalents. As much as they enjoy studying opportunities, the combination of perpetual unpreparedness and fear of losing their resources may ground Type Five investors on the sidelines. They would rather see their savings devalued by inflation than assume risks of capital losses.

KEY AVOIDANCE: REALITY CHECKS

The imaginary boundaries that Type Fives place on themselves, when taken to extremes, can result in reclusiveness and detachment from the outside world. Fearful Type Fives become out of touch with reality in their avoidance of allowing anyone or anything to influence their thoughts. Part of that aversion stems from a lack of confidence in their mental models, which are neither tried nor tested through vigorous exchanges with others. Ironically, the more Type Fives stay in their minds to feel secure in their learnings, the less competent they may become. Given how self-imposed exile and fear destroy individual confidence, more apprehension results.

CHIEF PROVOCATION: INCOMPETENCE

Because Type Fives do not wish to look or feel foolish, they may avoid making mistakes by stopping short of acting and sharing their thoughts with others. Without either, there is no error or risk of being judged. Actual competence in investing, however, can only be achieved through action with real money, not by writing memos or building hypothetical portfolios. In other words, the more Type Fives hold back from execution and connections, the less battle-tested they feel, which holds them back even more. Investing is a lifelong journey. Mistakes—provided they are not fatal to solvency—are valuable lessons essential to becoming better and more confident investors.

BLIND SPOT #1: EXTERNAL VIEWPOINTS

While blue-sky scenarios can easily sway Type Seven enthusiasts, and Type Six skeptics seek constant reassurances from others to assuage their anxieties, Type Fives tend to insulate themselves from external influences altogether. They may stick to what they are comfortable with and tune out other investment ideas, alternative theses, emerging trends, or disruptive technologies. If a Type Five investor prefers cash, everything else may be swiftly dismissed. If they are enamored with a stock, it is hard for anyone to introduce diversification or alternative asset classes. A Type Five investor's innate focus can turn into tunnel vision.

I am reminded of a story about a fund manager who held an interest in Redbox, an American DVD rental company with automated kiosks that were popular before the streaming era. In an interview years ago, that fund manager discussed his investment rationale behind Redbox with complete confidence. He declared how far into the weeds he was in all aspects of the company, including being able to recall how much each kiosk weighed, the replacement cycle, and the payback period. However, he missed the fact that video consumption was already shifting away from physical DVDs to streaming. Netflix was surging in popularity, and it would render Redbox kiosks obsolete. Yet his mind remained barricaded against an obvious secular change that would dismantle his entire investment thesis.

BLIND SPOT #2: HUMAN CONNECTION

The tendency to isolate deprives one of human connection, which is essential to reality checks and testing of investing ideas. Unhealthy Type Fives may not concur with this view. With a scarcity mindset, getting involved with others becomes a depletion of their energy reserves. In addition, forging relationships—even just professional collaborations—taps into their deep fears of dependency because they tend to regard people as unpredictable and demanding. Accordingly, solitude is a less painful option, and some Type Fives may justify their choices by believing their intellect to be incompatible with the masses. Since most people will reject intellectual snobs and recluses, it becomes a self-fulfilling prophecy.

TYPE FIVES:
WHEN DEALING WITH INVESTMENT
SUCCESSES AND FAILURES

The definition of investment success can differ from person to person. Most are satisfied with keeping pace with broader indices and prefer to stay within the pack. For those hyperfocused on capital conservation, success may mean zero capital losses, and Type Five investors shaped by scarcity mindsets are prone to thinking this way. Without capital risk, there can be no loss. If capital is deployed, it needs to be downside-protected. Type Fives may tell themselves there is no need to pursue anything more than token returns since their financial needs are economized to fit their narratives. To them, not losing is winning.

Type Fives who embrace investing may lean into the intellectual challenge of fringe assets. Micro-capitalization stocks or exotic alternative asset classes become captivating, while exchange-traded funds pegged to equity indices or fixed income may not present sufficient cerebral stimulation. If risky investments work out, returns can be enormous, in which case a Type Five investor will wade deeper into their internalized viewpoints.

On the other hand, if realities diverge from their investment theses, it may take a while for a Type Five's mental models to catch up with reality. A propensity to cling to their original conceptions and portfolio positions invariably inhibits change. Refusing help or advice is also likely since being rescued by anyone can suggest helplessness, which is a primal fear for Type Fives.

When bad investments with no hope of recovery fester in a portfolio, opportunity costs grow with time. The line between conviction and foolhardiness is thin, and Type Five investors risk not knowing which side of the line they stand on.

ROAD MAP
FOR TYPE FIVE INVESTORS

The key for Type Fives on their investing journey is leveraging their innate strengths—intellect, independent thinking, and focus—while establishing active guardrails to mitigate insular thinking, inertia, and isolation.

The first step is perhaps the most important, and the challenge is creating momentum to kick-start investing with an abundant mindset.

Finding the right trigger points that resonate with Type Five investors' natural rhythm is essential to making them jump onto the dance floor.

HOMEOWNERSHIP AND PRIVACY

Consistent with the Type Five need for privacy and space, an effective catalyst for personal investing is homeownership. Not having to share living quarters with parents or roommates is a compelling motivation for most investigators to part with their capital. Homeownership confers a safer, more secure abode than leasing. Type Fives must be vigilant of their natural tendency to seclude themselves, though, and not regress by erecting higher walls to keep people out.

KEEP THINGS IN MOTION WITH REGULAR INVESTMENT PLANS

To mitigate fears of being unprepared and looking foolish, Type Five investors can ease their investing journeys with regular investment into cost-effective exchange-traded funds covering stock indices and fixed income. Quantity is not as important as commencing the journey with quarterly or monthly capital outlays. Starting with exposure to established funds requires neither preparation nor research. Though it may not present Type Five investors with much intellectual challenge, the objective is to overcome hoarding and set things in motion.

ALWAYS PRACTICE DIVERSIFICATION

Once Type Fives dip a toe into the world of investing, the tendency to insulate and dig deep into their minds will take over sooner or later. To mitigate that, diversification is essential. Not only will Type Five investors enjoy the challenge of expanding their intellectual horizon, but a wide enough range of investments also forces them to avoid concentration risks around their most loved assets. No individual investment should exceed 2.5 percent of capital outlay, and there should be a low cap on the total capital allocated to stock picking, especially in the more speculative space and alternative investments. Much of a Type Five's portfolio should comprise home equity, real estate, and diversified index funds in equity and fixed income. With a portfolio spread across asset classes, industries, geographies, and individual positions, damage can be contained even if a Type Five is mentally trapped in certain investments facing diminishing prospects.

FORCE-SELL INDIVIDUAL INVESTMENTS ON SCHEDULE

The avaricious mindset of a Type Five may likely extend to clinging to portfolio positions. One of the key risks of investing outside of diversified ETFs is holding on to bad investments for far too long—or, worse, selling winners to double down on losers. This can happen to individual stocks, positions in cryptocurrencies, private investments in start-up ventures, derivatives, or even impaired investment properties. Cutting losses is difficult for any investor, especially those who insulate thinking to defend against reality or avoid the fear of feeling incompetent when taking stock of clunkers.

Consequently, a fixed schedule to force-sell investments may be a practical forcing function for Type Five investors. Think of it as a spring-cleaning exercise to shake up an investment portfolio periodically. Weeding out investments that have deviated too far from their original theses will also allow for capital to be recycled. This exercise requires an external Marie Kondo–like figure for inputs; otherwise, Type Five investors may remain unyielding in their heads.

SEEK INVESTMENT ADVICE

Collaboration may be difficult for Type Fives who are used to self-sufficiency, but it is essential. Finding the right investing partners offers opportunities to retest investment theses and make them better. Financial advisers may provide different ideas for building retirement portfolios. Such parties need not be from existing social or professional circles. Joining specific investment communities allows one to investigate how alternative portfolio constructs perform in real time. Accessing professional analysts or industry experts with the proper credentials can help enrich learning. These are some possible options to serve as a counterweight against the odds of Type Five investors getting too wrapped up in their parochial visions.

The right partners should challenge Type Five investors and their thinking. Nothing is a sure bet; again, we do not know what we do not know. Even the most knowledgeable Type Five investors are fallible, liable to get trapped in their own convictions. They must also realize that everyone needs help on the investing journey and relying on partnerships or professional advice does not suggest incompetence, a core fear of Type Fives.

BEWARE OF VALUE TRAPS

Type Fives tend to minimize their needs in order to conserve time and resources. This preservation tactic can seep into their investment mentality as well. Type Five investors may correlate seemingly high valuation multiples with excesses and dismiss every investment opportunity that does not appear cheap. Warren Buffet once said, "It is far better to buy a wonderful company at a fair price than a fair company at a wonderful price." Quality companies rarely trade at a discount.

Conversely, cheap assets can be value traps for Type Fives. If a Type Five investor becomes too fixated on finding bargains and overlooks red flags that point to the fundamental deterioration of value, it becomes easy to be ensnarled. Unless there is mass panic in a bear market, assets trade at a discount for a reason, and Type Five investors must resist the temptation to be cheap.

DEVELOPMENT PLAN FOR FIVES: INTEGRATING TOWARD TYPE SEVEN (ENTHUSIAST) AND TYPE EIGHT (CHALLENGER)

> "Forget the book. Trust your instincts. Don't think. Just do. You think up there, you're dead. Believe me."
> *Top Gun: Maverick (2022)*

Captain Pete "Maverick" Mitchell might as well be speaking directly to Type Fives in the above lines from the *Top Gun* sequel. Played by Tom Cruise, Maverick is an excellent aviator but prone to recklessness. He is also a flight instructor to Lieutenant Bradley "Rooster" Bradshaw, who is almost the antithesis of Maverick and repeatedly holds himself back as a pilot until the film's end.

Maverick is a Type Eight personality, driven by instinct, and does not hesitate to act. Impulsive as his character may be, he also displays complete mastery of aviation skills and intimate knowledge of his aircraft. Maverick trusts his gut to take decisive actions when life and death hang in the balance. His dire warning against overthinking in critical situations is a valuable message to the overly cerebral types. The predisposition to retreat into the safety of the mind may buy Type Fives some security, but complete inaction comes at a cost.

Reflecting on the why behind that constant inclination to detach from the real world is essential in any Type Five personal development plan. Justifying isolation with reasons like superior intellect or needing space to think may be valid, but it can also be an ego defense to hang on to familiar coping mechanisms.

According to Enneagram theory, Type Five investigators may not have felt sufficiently protected and nurtured by their caretakers growing up. Without dependable sources of soothing and security, they learn not to seek them and instead find solace in intellectualization. A firm stance on self-sufficiency then develops to counter their fears of being let down by others again; hence, avoiding relationships becomes a way of protecting their inner fragility.

This upbringing defines a Type Five psyche and influences all aspects of life. Anytime there is uncertainty, an unconscious crutch is triggered, and Type Fives withdraw into their minds to disconnect from emotional needs. Learning to feel safe with people and trust the world is critical to resolving unfinished business from childhood. This does not imply a childlike naivete but rather a mixture of healthy skepticism with an open mind and courage.

The Type Seven enthusiast archetype presents a stretch model for the mind. Though belonging to the same head triad as Type Five investigators, the best enthusiasts have no fear of the external world, harboring neither distrust nor a perpetual sense of unpreparedness as they jump into each experience. Rather than worrying about being fatigued by people, Type Sevens embrace connections and view human interactions as energy sources. Isolation is not the only way to recharge one's mind.

Breaking out of self-imposed boundaries with the courage of a Type Eight challenger is another pivot for Type Fives. Liberation is possible when these thinkers believe viscerally in their power and take up space in the world. Type Eights epitomize the strength of self-belief, demonstrated outward in their conquests. When Type Fives are intentional with the same boldness and action bias, predilections to overthink will unclench over time.

Freed from overthinking, Type Five investors adopt a fluid balance between contemplation and actual capital deployment. Neither holding back due to fears nor clinging to a hoarding mindset, they take measured risks. Portfolio allocations are diversified and not skewed toward the esoteric or fringe. Open minds bond with changing realities rather than defending against them. There is no concern about feeling foolish when admitting mistakes and pivoting away from prior convictions. All the while, these Type Five investors are collaborative, energized by exchanges with the outside world.

When no longer confined in their heads, the best investigators can still be as cerebral as Sherlock Holmes, but they also push the throttle to take flight into the world.

Chapter 8

Type Six: Maurizio Gucci (of *House of Gucci*)

When the 2021 film *House of Gucci* came out, almost all the attention was focused on Lady Gaga (especially her Italian accent) and how she immersed herself in the role of Patrizia Reggiani. She was front and center in the publicity campaign, garnering the most award nominations out of all the actors attached to the project. No small feat, considering the star-studded ensemble that includes Academy Award–winning actors Al Pacino, Jeremy Irons, and Jared Leto.

Lost somewhere in that hype was Adam Driver and his portrayal of Maurizio Gucci, a character equally pivotal to the film as the one played by Lady Gaga. Both characters undergo extreme transitions in the story: Maurizio starts off as a meek aspiring lawyer and becomes a conniving usurper of his uncle's stake in Gucci; Patrizia, as Lady Gaga described metaphorically, transforms from a house cat into a murderous panther.

Underneath all those designer outfits, I would argue that Maurizio Gucci undergoes a more radical character makeover in the script than Patrizia Reggiani does. He begins as a shy, risk-averse individual who enjoys studying books on Italy's legislative process. Maurizio lives at home with an overprotective father, who controls a 50 percent interest in Gucci, but does not wish anything to do with the family business, preferring to strike out on his own.

Until he meets Patrizia Reggiani.

In spite (or perhaps because) of objections from his father, Maurizio falls in love with Patrizia. Maurizio proceeds to leave home and walk away from his inheritance. In addition, he discontinues his studies to work at his father-in-law's transportation company. Talk about doing a 180, and this is just in the first innings of the film. Patrizia, on the other hand, remains a feline go-getter from start to finish; she just becomes more vicious.

Maurizio is a Type Six skeptic, and he undergoes the full passage of personality development via his relationship with Patrizia. Lured by the prospect of a stable, loving union with his future wife, Maurizio first finds the courage to break away from his overbearing father. Years later, however, Maurizio begins to doubt his marriage. Patrizia calls him a cretin as the first signs of instability arise between them. She is depicted as a strong-willed but divisive force, sowing discord between Maurizio and his wider family network instead of bringing the family closer together. Consequently, Maurizio's sense of security in his marriage falters, and emotional uncertainty builds. Her meddling in the family business also undermines his sense of competence.

Maurizio capitulates the moment he meets Paola Franchi, an attractive upper-class friend from his schooling years. He develops a new personal support network with Paola, not unlike how he initially swaps his father for Patrizia. There is no break between marriage and his new relationship with Paolo; he couples up even before his marriage is legally dissolved. Neither is there a hint of guilt for leaving his wife and daughter.

Ironically, Maurizio's archetypal determination to move toward safety by removing Patrizia from his life leads to his demise.

Note to self: Never mess with a feline go-getter!

PERSONALITY OF TYPE SIXES (SKEPTICS)

Type Sixes are primarily motivated by security. They want to feel supported, and they believe in the status quo for as long as it feels reassuring. No wonder these personalities are also known as "skeptics" and "loyalists" in the Enneagram world. Socially, they enjoy long-standing relationships with family and friends; professionally, many Type Sixes find long and steady employment within large organizations.

A deep desire for security also compels these skeptics to think of multiple ways it can be compromised. Contingency planning, worst-case-scenario analyses, and insurance policies are standard tools to prevent or mitigate adverse outcomes in almost every aspect of their lives. Consequently, Type Sixes tend to be meticulous, vigilant, and diligent. However, the underlying wariness against danger (real or imagined) can result in significant anxiousness. Anxiety is a primary trait for this personality type, whether in good or bad times.

In dealing with uncertainties, Type Sixes will vacillate for extended periods for two reasons. First, they want to consider multiple paths to resolving uncertainties; each option must be assessed carefully for upside and downside risks. Second, skeptics will also reach out to others—usually people they trust and respect—to seek their opinions and thoughts. Oddly enough, the more alternatives and viewpoints are considered, the more anxious they may become. For a Type Six, doubt is a constant, and making up one's mind can be difficult, especially if the stakes are high.

Their attitude toward relationships can be contradictory. Even though they crave reliable integrity in their respective systems (workplace, family, community, partnership, friendship), their fluttering minds cannot help but question the basis of trust invested in individuals and groups. This tension creates a constant state of apprehension, prompting either defensive actions (for example, seeking reassurance and undertaking risk-mitigation measures) or offensive deeds (which can be in the form of rebellion or sudden capitulations)—or both.

In summary, a central theme for Type Sixes is polarity. They can be loyal and disloyal, abiding and nonabiding, believing and disbelieving, defensive and offensive, trusting and distrusting, assured and suspicious, and so on. Their need for a strong support network—including solid personal bonds, stable organizations, and reliable mentorship—paradoxically takes them further away from what they need the most: self-confidence. The more they depend on external structures and third parties to derive security, the less independent they become. Anxiety will continue to define them until they find the confidence to trust themselves.

The healthiest Type Sixes are those who have developed self-reliance. Sufficient faith in oneself is the antidote to stress, indecisiveness, and the need for constant reassurance. We can see that demonstrated by Maurizio Gucci in the film. At his best, he forms a strategic alliance with Investcorp to seize control of Gucci from his uncle and cousin. Once in charge, he is unafraid to overhaul the business, including hiring a new creative director (Tom Ford) to take the brand in an entirely different direction. He grows so bold he even appropriates corporate funds to fund his lifestyle. That last bit got him removed from Gucci, but we digress. Maurizio's character transformation demonstrates the entire Type Six continuum of personality development, culminating in him standing toe-to-toe with a private equity giant and taking charge of the family business he initially rejects out of fear.

One wonders what else Maurizio Gucci would have accomplished had Patrizia Reggiani not abruptly ended his journey. Then again, the film *House of Gucci* would not exist.

CHECKLIST FOR TYPE SIX

If you respond "Yes" to, or resonate with, most of the questions and the statements below, you are likely to be a Type Six:

- ☐ When assigned new responsibilities at work, you are more likely to view them as additional sources of anxiety than an opportunity to outshine your peers.
- ☐ Before making important decisions, you tend to first seek guidance and reassurance from people you trust rather than figuring them out on your own.
- ☐ You tend to purchase goods and services—including groceries, legal advice, medical care, fashion apparel, and electronics—almost exclusively from well-known brands because you trust them rather than experiment with newer, lesser-known names.
- ☐ At work, if you sense a lack of support from colleagues or superiors, you are more likely to feel discouraged than motivated to prove yourself to them.
- ☐ Working in a small, unknown start-up does not excite or interest you because you prefer the certainty and security of large, branded organizations.
- ☐ When analyzing problems—at work or in your personal life—you like to consider multiple upside and downside scenarios, each with its own set of variables, and hence, you often find it hard to make up your mind.
- ☐ Between "What can go wrong?" and "What can go right?" the former resonates stronger with you.
- ☐ You pride yourself on having a solid support network

of friends and family and often update them on every significant development in your life.
- ☐ Between following rules and finding loopholes to your advantage, you resonate more with the former.
- ☐ You continually evaluate your friends based on whom you can trust and cannot, even those you have known for years.

TYPE SIX INVESTORS

Putting money at risk may seem like the last thing Type Six personalities want. Why endanger their security by taking money out of the bank—where it is truly safe—and subject it to the whipsaws of market forces? Already, a Type Six is inclined to be in a state of polarity, shuffling back and forth between opposing thoughts; adding on worries that come with putting money to work may seem like a mental burden not worth having.

Regarding financial health, primary reliance on a paycheck for livelihood is inherently an uneasy proposition for any Type Six; they will never feel secure in the long run. In other words, financial independence for a Type Six is the ultimate promised land. Only then will they feel safe. To get there, one needs to start investing early; the road to heaven is paved with trials and tribulations.

CORE MOTIVATION: TO BE SAFE

Type Six investors seek safety in everything, including financial decisions. It does not mean they cannot invest, but they need to feel secure before taking action with their money. Type Sixes who are less informed about financial planning or the importance of building a retirement portfolio may choose to do nothing, preferring the comfort of knowing exactly how much they have in the bank, even if the value of money is eroded by inflation. The baseline is always to shield themselves from the forces of demand and supply. Fear of the unknown is a deterrence for many Type Sixes; hence, inaction becomes a default choice.

Some Type Six investors may have no tolerance for debt, so they strive to eliminate the chances of incurring any financial default. In certain circumstances, such prudence is a virtue and prevents one from taking on credit card debt to go on indulgent shopping sprees. Using all excess cash to pay off expensive student loans can also make sense. On the other hand, if that aversion amplifies and they refuse to take up even low-cost mortgages to fund modest home purchases they can afford, then that virtue becomes a handicap.

Type Six investors active in financial planning will almost always gravitate toward more secure asset classes, but subjectivity comes into play here. Some may view American dollars as the steadiest form of asset. Others will think gold to be the most dependable; after all, wars have been waged over this prized metal since time immemorial. Or they may put all their money into real estate, the world's largest asset class. Safety in numbers confers a deep sense of security.

PRIMARY INFATUATION: WORST-CASE SCENARIOS

Alongside Type Five investigators and Type Seven enthusiasts, Type Sixes belong to the head triad of the Enneagram, and they are driven by their intellect. Unlike Type Sevens, who can be easily swayed by blue-sky scenarios, or Type Fives, who are rooted in their own minds, Type Six investors examine a spectrum of possible outcomes when assessing investment opportunities. Because they always have lingering doubts, they are cautious and tend to ask for external opinions to test theirs.

Skepticism in a healthy dose can be a powerful tool in personal investing, preventing one from getting swept up in a bull market. When taken too far, it becomes paranoia, and Type Six investors may only focus on what can go wrong. Extreme caution can keep them from ever deploying cash into anything other than, say, savings bonds. If they do have money invested, any bearishness in prevailing market sentiment may cause them to capitulate on their riskier assets. Premature selling can come at a high price, measured in the upside forgone out of fear.

KEY AVOIDANCE: BEING THE LONE VOICE IN THE ROOM

Type Six investors are usually not the ones to back early-stage companies (unless they find safety in numbers co-investing with large institutions) or to be contrarians. They may avoid situations in which they feel their viewpoints are unsupported by others. This has several implications for their investment approaches. They are likely drawn only to investments others have validated, hence real estate, index funds, and large capitalization corporations are attractive destinations. In real estate, for example, Type Six investors may only direct their capital toward residential properties located in established areas, staying clear of unfamiliar territories.

CHIEF PROVOCATION: LACK OF SUPPORT

Because Type Six investors find safety in numbers, capitulation becomes likely when market tides turn against them and they are made to feel like they are the ones left holding the bag. Doubt fills their minds quicker than it does other archetypes; without safety in numbers, downside scenarios may overwhelm their thinking.

Take Tesla as an example. In May 2019, Morgan Stanley issued an updated research report with an eye-catching bear-case price target of $10 per share. That was presplit, and the stock was trading at around $200, a three-year low. Investors were essentially warned of a possible wipeout, with concerns around Chinese demand for Tesla products cited as a critical reason for the worst-case scenario. In the first half of 2019, Tesla was still in production hell. SEC fraud charges against cofounder Elon Musk, though settled, remained topical. Famous fund managers David Einhorn and Jim Chanos were decrying the stock on CNBC to support their shorts. Negativity on Tesla was in vogue. In such an unsupportive environment, Type Six investors holding Tesla would likely have folded just before the stock appreciated multifold throughout 2020 and 2021.

BLIND SPOT #1: BEST-CASE SCENARIOS

Personal investing requires fundamental faith that the future will be better than the present—that portfolio valuation will at least outpace inflation to create a financial safety net at retirement. If an apocalyptic future awaits, everyone should live in the present and forget about delaying gratification. Type Six investors who focus too much on downside risks may be underestimating their ability to take control of their financial future. That is fine if they still deploy capital toward safer asset classes. However, if everything is hoarded in cash, it will be detrimental to their finances—due to inflation—and their self-confidence.

BLIND SPOT #2: TRUST IN THEMSELVES AND OTHERS

Perhaps the greatest irony of Type Six investors is that their unconscious quest for external support systems and reassurance may further undermine the value of their individual views and confidence to sustain them. The more they rely on validation, the less able they become to develop unique perspectives that can stand independently from others. To build self-confidence, separation from the crowd is essential. Type Sixes must consciously lean into self-determination in thinking and action. That said, taking premature leaps of faith that do not end well may have the counterproductive effect of permanently putting them off taking risks altogether.

TYPE SIXES:
WHEN DEALING WITH INVESTMENT
SUCCESSES AND FAILURES

For Type Six investors, even investment successes might not bolster self-confidence. This is because, mentally, they tend to identify more with self-doubt, which can amplify when encountering inevitable stumbles in any personal investing journey. Additionally, sustainable investment success requires tolerating uncertainties (and volatilities) for long periods, despite what may happen to the broader economy or the world. Whether making a sensible home purchase and watching the housing market subsequently wobble or investing periodically in an index fund as markets gyrate like Jennifer Lopez in *Hustlers* (2019), for investments to bear fruits, the process demands patience, consistency, and endurance. Type Six investors must endeavor to observe their anxieties and self-doubt without giving up prematurely. They must stay on track long enough to witness positive results and then learn to attribute those results to their own efficacy.

Compared to the more insular Type Fives and the ever-optimistic Type Sevens, Type Sixes are prone to quickly question their rationale if asset prices move against them. This may prompt them to change course at inopportune times. When COVID-19 hit and precipitated a free fall in prices across almost all asset classes, stories of people getting out of stocks ran rampant, with many taking losses. Markets, however, recovered quickly. Diving in and out of assets out of fear is a recipe for disaster since that usually results in buying high and selling low.

ROAD MAP FOR TYPE SIX INVESTORS

The key to investing for Type Six investors is anxiety management. If uncomfortable risks are taken at the start of one's investing journey and asset prices go awry too soon—which almost always happens—a Type Six investor may become motivated to eliminate the anxiety and give up altogether. It may take years for that Type Six investor to regain boldness before taking more portfolio actions. For some, personal investing may not ever resume.

On the other hand, starting conservatively—both in choices of investment assets and quantity—will allow Type Six investors to build more self-confidence before graduating to either larger deployments or higher-risk categories and to make money work a little harder. Structure, pace, and regularity are therefore crucial for Type Six investors; simplicity should be the bedrock principle.

The naturally meticulous and vigilant Type Six personalities have the makings of excellent investors. Their ability to comb through upside and downside scenarios, assess risk exposures, and monitor changing investment theses are intellectual skills that will serve them well in the long run.

AIM FOR HOMEOWNERSHIP

Overpaying or overleveraging aside, homeownership is well suited to a Type Six mentality. Not only is real estate the largest asset class in the world—hence safety in numbers—but homes are tangible assets that can provide proprietors with round-the-clock, multisensory assurance. Since Type Sixes tend to be cautious, they can trust themselves to make well-considered choices when purchasing their first homes, but they must still make a move.

A Type Six investor will appreciate the regularity at which the mortgage is paid down and equity built up over time. It is also a great way to establish fiscal discipline early in one's career. Perhaps the most significant benefit to Type Six investors is a unique sense of self-possession that is worth more than any financial merit.

FOCUS MORE ON REAL ESTATE

Since many Type Six investors enjoy long, steady employment in large organizations and are likely to have good credit scores to secure better mortgage rates, they can consider making real estate a pivotal anchor to their portfolios.

Perception-wise, real estate assets do not present the same level of volatility as other investment classes quoted on exchanges. Property owners do not wake up each morning to get the latest Zestimate, unlike many equity investors who check stock prices more often than that. Additionally, the tangible nature of properties provides a unique layer of security for anxious minds. There is something to be said about investment assets that you can see and touch. To a Type Six investor, it matters.

DIVERSIFY WITH LOWER-RISK EXCHANGE-TRADED FUNDS

The idea here is to broaden portfolio exposures in stealth mode over multiple market cycles without arousing anxieties. After homeownership is established, Type Six investors may consider establishing automatic monthly or quarterly deployments into ETFs that offer diversification into stocks and fixed income. The choice of funds, at least at the beginning of one's investment journey, must be rooted in conservativeness. The objective is to ensure Type Six investors do not hit the eject button during market volatility. The invested amount should also be small at the start so that extreme price movements will not move the needle on aggregate portfolio value already anchored by real estate.

AVOID HIGH-RISK ASSETS

To a Type Six investor, exposure to extreme volatility is like adding fuel to a wildfire. It is counterproductive, especially at the start of one's investment journey when a Type Six investor needs to pick up momentum without the risk of muddling the end goal. For example, buying a nonfungible token that gives a stake in that digital tiara might sound so meta, but price fluctuations will give Type Six investors splitting headaches in the real world. There is no point in making random bets, either. Buying 0.00001 of a Bitcoin, just because everyone else is doing it, will not move the needle; the volatility will only distract a Six investor from developing a concrete and systematic game plan.

MAKE FINANCIAL PLANNING A GROUP ACTIVITY

In accordance with their natural tendencies to seek advice and safety in numbers, Type Six investors should consider turning to their spouses, families, or friends to make financial planning a group activity. Dealing with hard-earned money can be intimidating, especially at the start of one's career, but early anxieties can be managed by tapping on the right people for support and advice. Working in teams, which is how Type Six personalities like it, leads to higher odds of reaching the promised land of financial independence. Type Six investors should discuss portfolio planning with trusted individuals within their social and professional circles or consider appointing third-party financial advisers.

CAUTIOUS APPROACH TO INDIVIDUAL STOCK PICKING

Individual stocks of large companies may be the next step in financial planning. Even at scale, big technology giants can still outperform the market. Witness the continued growth of Microsoft and Apple after exceeding the $1 trillion mark in market capitalizations, but with less volatility relative to smaller peers. Type Six investors can flex their mature investing muscles by adding individual names to their equity portfolios once they gain sufficient confidence in their financial security.

DEVELOPMENT PLAN FOR SIXES: INTEGRATING TOWARD TYPE THREE (PERFORMER) AND TYPE NINE (PEACEMAKER)

If Maurizio Gucci had not been murdered and had sold his 50 percent Gucci stake to Investcorp for $150 million, he would have been a formidable investor. It is an extrapolation, but this hypothetical exercise may be informative. I imagine Maurizio would not just keep the $150 million in the bank out of fear of taking risks or anxiety about not knowing what to do with it. Instead, he might seed new investments—after, of course, more personal indulgences like another Lamborghini—that align with his passion and vision. He would neither focus only on run-of-the-mill asset classes nor make hasty punts on seductive but high-risk bets. Though anxiety would still be part of his human condition, it might not define him anymore. Instead, Maurizio, the investor, would be grounded by self-trust and supported by a reliable network of carefully chosen advisers.

Striking a balance between independent thinking and relevant perspectives from outsiders, Maurizio would meticulously calculate the odds of success with each investment opportunity without undue hesitation that might hold him back from taking decisive actions. Doubt would be addressed and measured but not allowed to fester into overarching apprehension. I reckon his late 1990s and early 2000s portfolio could include part LVMH (Louis Vuitton Möet Hennessy), part luxury real estate, with a dash of seed money in up-and-coming fashion labels. Maurizio would also call his own shots, with precise foresight and the courage to be different.

The image above shows a healthy Type Six investor who has broken out of a cycle of debilitating internal doubt and attachment to external approval. Maurizio Gucci's story spans decades, and his character evolution does not happen overnight, even though 158 minutes of screen time may make it appear so.

It is not a coincidence that the most significant changes to Maurizio's early adulthood, as depicted in the film, were catalyzed by his relationship with Patrizia Reggiani, an archetypal Type Three. She brings her go-getter, take-no-prisoners personality into the marriage and pushes Maurizio to fight for his fair share of the Gucci empire. Rather than pursuing a safe career in law or driving trucks, Maurizio is propelled into an upward climb at Gucci that takes him on an inadvertent Type Three development course. When his marriage becomes rocky, Maurizio overhauls his personal life to resolve his growing anxiety with Patrizia by establishing a new but stable union with Paola Franchi. This is essentially a Type Nine pivot.

Type Six prototypes are plagued by self-doubt, preventing them from making the daring decisions necessary to build self-confidence. Reliance on direction and support from others likely originated from their formative years when they were deeply connected to their protective figures, perhaps in the form of overly watchful mothers or fathers. Rather than developing a sense of agency, they perceived the right actions as the ones advised by those adults hovering over them. It then becomes habitual to be on a constant lookout for guidance since self-sufficiency has not been given any meaningful space or time to compound. Making independent decisions when they come of age thus becomes challenging. As adults, Type Sixes continue to look for similar caretaking figures in their employers, partners, counselors, and friends to provide reassurance and corroboration.

Type Six investors must accumulate confidence slowly and take charge of their financial future. Without a systematic plan to build stand-alone financial portfolios of their own, their relationship with money will be a tenuous one. Type Six investors who rely solely on employment to sustain their livelihoods are more likely to be subject to a constant flux between wanting to break away from single points of failure and fears of taking risks with their capital. Only by embarking on sustained investment journeys will Type Sixes truly address their inherent anxiety and grow in confidence to establish their own safety nets.

Chapter 9

Type Seven:
Freddie Mercury (of *Bohemian Rhapsody*)

> "Freddie, you're burning the candle at both ends!"
> "Yes, but the glow is so divine."
> ***Bohemian Rhapsody* (2018)**

In a pivotal scene from the movie *Bohemian Rhapsody,* Mary Austin visits her best friend Freddie Mercury in Germany, where he is recording his solo album. She is shocked to find him asleep on a sofa, surrounded by remnants of a wild house party. With a mix of frustration and compassion, Austin implores an exhausted Mercury to slow down and return to England, as life abroad appears chaotic. The house is full of knocked-over glasses, scattered cocaine, bottles of alcohol, and piles of cigarettes. His life in Germany is awash in debauchery and an endless stream of fans (and groupies) who fawn all over him. Despite abundant financial means and constant company, he is depicted as desperate and forlorn.

The scene is clear: Freddie Mercury is entirely out of control at this point in his life.

Contrast this to earlier scenes in the movie showing him and his Queen bandmates producing their masterpiece album, *A Night at the Opera*. That version of Mercury is in his element—confident, experimental, and invigorating. He taps into the past as part of his creative process. Instead of burying painful memories, he finds quiet moments to reach deep and writes his most famous single, "Bohemian Rhapsody." That song is solely credited to him, and its profound lyrics reference his personal traumas. In one scene, Mercury tears up while composing the tune on his piano in solitude. Combining seemingly disparate musical structures with novel production techniques, "Bohemian Rhapsody" immortalizes the singer as a genius.

This is Freddie Mercury at his best, glowing from the inside, and not from substances.

Bohemian Rhapsody chronicles the singer's journey from his early days as a baggage handler at Heathrow Airport to his triumphant performance with Queen at Live Aid 1985. The film also happens to be a character study of a Type Seven (enthusiast).

While developing the movie, the producers wanted the script to focus more on Freddie Mercury the singer and songwriter than the closeted rock star who died of AIDS in 1991. At the same time, the storyline does not shy away from portraying his vulnerabilities, starting with his relationship with his father. From an early age, Mercury—born Farrokh Bulsara—is intent on escaping his Parsi-Indian roots to embrace rock and roll. He is met with constant disapproval from his traditional-minded father. Their tenuous relationship is evident minutes into the film; both reject each other. Mercury also struggles with his sexual identity and the protruding appearance of his teeth.

Consistent with a Type Seven archetype, the singer distracts from his emotional tumult with over-the-top antics onstage and off, but he produces some of his best songs when he tunes into his feelings and engages in rigorous collaborations with his bandmates. Unmatched musical talent and charisma make Freddie Mercury a legend. However, his emotional journey to healing in *Bohemian Rhapsody* is concluded with far fewer theatrics: in a simple hug between father and son. This seems to fill a void in Mercury's heart that no worldly accomplishment could have.

PERSONALITY OF TYPE SEVENS
(ENTHUSIASTS)

Type Sevens are also known as the "enthusiasts," the "adventurers," and the "dreamers." This Enneagram archetype is characterized by unbound energy and an insatiable taste for stimulation. They are rarely alone as they love the company of friends, family, colleagues, and even strangers. Think of fun-loving, life-of-the-party people with plenty of great stories to tell and enough spontaneity to inspire an entire room. Type Sevens embrace life by seemingly living it to the fullest, and many of them enjoy consuming all they can get their hands on, from vacations to fine art and wines. World economies depend on these enthusiasts to ward off recessions.

Beneath the surface lies a keen intellect. Despite appearances, Type Sevens belong to the same head triad as the more subdued Type Five investigators and the hesitant Type Six skeptics. All of them have curious minds, but what sets the enthusiasts apart is their willingness to hurl themselves into experiences. When quick minds are paired with energetic actions, Type Sevens learn much faster. The best Type Sevens are not mere consumers but are also relentless creators driven by original ideas and visions for the future. They include renowned visionaries like Richard Branson, Steven Spielberg, and Mozart.

Fear is the flip side of intellect in the head triad, and each archetype copes differently. Consistent with their outward projection of vigor, Type Sevens tend to avoid fear by relying on stimuli derived from external sources, which can range from adventurous travel and entrepreneurship to new relationships and copious consumption. In contrast, Type Fives typically pull back into the comfort of their minds, and Type Sixes oscillate between seeking external assurance and listening to their inner voices to manage fear.

Enthusiasm for more, when taken too far, can become an addiction. Unhealthy Type Sevens often avoid emotional discomfort through busyness, expending their energies everywhere except inwardly. Introspection and reflection are rare since the unconscious motive is to avoid connecting with painful feelings buried deep in their psyches. Accordingly, the mind and body are kept active, lurching toward more elaborate stimulation. But unhealthy enthusiasts are never really sated since their true desires can only be uncovered when they untangle their hearts.

On the other hand, well-developed Type Sevens do not regard their inner worlds with aversion. They are attuned to their feelings, not just euphoria but the whole spectrum of human emotions, displaying the same intellectual curiosity inwardly and outwardly. Simplistic experiences can be equally refreshing since their minds are in the present to absorb every detail.

Recall Mercury's emotional journey at the end of *Bohemian Rhapsody* when he returns to America to reunite with his bandmates. No more hedonistic parties or excesses: He lives alone, accepts the fragility of his physical condition, commits to a low-key relationship, and devotes himself to rehearsals. In addition, the singer shares a touching moment with his father, who finally accepts Farrokh Bulsara as Freddie Mercury, acknowledging his good thoughts, good words, and good deeds at Live Aid.

CHECKLIST FOR TYPE SEVEN

If you respond "Yes" to, or resonate with, most of the questions and the statements below, you are likely to be a Type Seven:

- ☐ Compared to your peers, you possess more personal items, like electronics, clothing, and fashion accessories.

- ☐ In group settings, you feed off the energy of others and enjoy enthralling people with stories of your adventures.
- ☐ YOLO ("You only live once") is a phrase that resonates.
- ☐ Being alone does not happen frequently, as your professional and personal calendars are full of activities with multiple parties.
- ☐ Everyday routine gets boring quickly.
- ☐ You possess vast knowledge across various subjects, partly because you have a good memory and learn fast.
- ☐ Being spontaneous is second nature to you; when you want to do something, you jump into it with little to no hesitation.
- ☐ You embrace life to the fullest, from professional endeavors and side projects to travel, food, and books.
- ☐ When evaluating business plans or investment opportunities, you get more excited by the possibilities of upside and may spend less time contemplating what can go wrong.
- ☐ Introspection and prolonged contemplation of your emotions are rare.

TYPE SEVEN INVESTORS

When strategically aligned, the combination of a formidable mind, thirst for knowledge, propensity for action, and energetic networking can equal success in any endeavor, including personal investing. Type Sevens have what it takes to accomplish any task, but only if they do not go overboard. Compared with the overthinking Type Fives and hesitant Type Sixes, Type Sevens have the opposite problem, whether taking on too much risk exposure, being too impatient, or attempting too many changes to their portfolio. Appreciating the concept of less is more is key to their road map.

Likewise, exercising fiscal discipline to allocate resources toward long-term investments and away from current consumption may challenge Type Sevens, who do not like to feel deprived. Therefore, negotiating the tension between a dopamine fix through being limitless and accepting self-restraint is critical.

CORE MOTIVATIONS: TO MAKE BIGGER AND BOLDER BETS

The insatiable appetite of Type Sevens applies to the whole nine yards, from having the most incredible experiences to acquiring more friends and knowledge. It also affects how they approach personal investing. Type Seven investors can get carried away when ideas "spark joy." They may jump from opportunity to opportunity, wanting to invest in everything. A portfolio full of disparate positions can result.

Type Seven investors may also be swayed by asymmetrical returns, looking for that elusive jackpot without sufficiently considering potential risks. Consistent with the pleasure principle, they may be drawn to gambles masquerading as exciting investments. The anticipation of a significant payoff to fuel their imagined future is almost irresistible. Making large bets is a strong likelihood, especially if early investments turn out well by strokes of luck. Success breeds an addictive cycle of looking for the next big hit.

PRIMARY INFATUATION: ROSE-TINTED FUTURE

Blue-sky investment cases will appeal to Type Seven investors. This makes high-growth, speculative assets and early-stage ventures incredibly enticing because many of these investments require investors to imagine what could go right instead of what could go wrong. Enthusiasts are not inclined to think of downside cases, nor do they want to. The more outlandish and bullish the upside scenarios, the more fascinated Type Seven investors will be. Floating islands in international waters, space travel, and terraforming Mars are some ideas to draw these enthusiastic investors like a moth to the flame.

KEY AVOIDANCE: PAINFUL INVESTMENT PROCESSES

Type Sevens are often in a hurry to move forward because staying in the present to deal with mundane details (or reality) can be painful, and they have little to no inherent interest in doing so. When it comes to investing, performing proper due diligence can be long and arduous. There is a reason why corporations tend to have layers of approval committees, requiring written memos and group discussions to unpack ideas before major resources are approved for deployment.

Pain avoidance in Type Sevens can result in rash investment choices. They may skim through information and make snap decisions. A hypothetical scenario might be "This electric vehicle start-up sounds awesome; I am in." Due diligence on the business plan, multiple-scenario analyses, investigation into the founder-management team, questions on cash burn, and study of potential production capabilities are likely sped through or swept away by excitement.

CHIEF PROVOCATION: LIMITATIONS

Nothing triggers Type Sevens more than limitations. Restraints, when enforced externally, are likely to provoke quick reactions. Borrowing becomes tempting when they run out of capital to invest or realize there is insufficient cash after all that spending. Using complex derivatives—financial instruments that magnify risks and returns—to free oneself of capital limitations becomes another enticing (and high-risk) option by which to chase those big returns.

BLIND SPOT #1: BEAR CASES

The combination of rose-tinted lenses and an intense urgency to move toward the future can lead to scant attention paid to alternative viewpoints and downside cases. Or Sevens may just tune them out altogether. Things can always go wrong; even dominant corporations sometimes slip into oblivion over time due to disruptive technologies, shifting paradigms, or changing consumer tastes. Think General Electric and Kodak. Part of the curse of being intellectually confident—and many Type Sevens are—is that it becomes difficult to step away from one's conviction to contemplate antitheses. A portfolio heavy on speculations and lacking in lower-risk asset classes such as diversified funds, fixed income, and cash becomes likely.

BLIND SPOT #2: OVERNIGHT EXPERTISE CAN BE INCOMPLETE

Because Type Sevens assimilate and retain information quickly, they have a lower learning curve than any other Enneagram type. These enthusiasts may believe themselves to be overnight experts through a combination of quick thinking and fervent doing. That said, they can also get bored and move on to something else altogether just as quickly to seek more mental stimulation before attaining true expertise. A jack-of-all-trades phenomenon may result.

As Malcolm Gladwell once said, achieving true mastery takes 10,000 hours of work. When it comes to investing, enthusiasts may assume they have already learned enough and declare their meteoric rise with trademark optimism. Quick decisions follow, and if the stakes are too high and luck is not on their side, costly mistakes result.

TYPE SEVENS: WHEN DEALING WITH INVESTMENT SUCCESSES AND FAILURES

In processing an investing journey, many Type Seven investors rationalize the ups and downs in ways that mirror their personality traits. When investments work out brilliantly, typical enthusiasts will be emboldened and unconsciously feed off the highs. This triggers a new cycle of desire for more, resulting in a larger risk appetite. Rose-tinted glasses get rosier as Type Sevens become more convinced of their expertise, even if luck has played a significant role.

Unhealthy Type Seven investors are hence susceptible to getting swept up by bull market fever. When they are not conscious of the downside and alternative perspectives, they may be prone to doubling down at peak prices and increasing risk exposure at precisely the wrong time. Lack of discipline and skepticism and an affinity for nonstop action are ingredients for a feeding frenzy that can end in tears. Healthy Type Seven investors, by contrast, exercise far more restraint with their capital and do not get carried away by external stimuli or blind faith.

When it comes to failed investments, Type Sevens may not be accustomed to confronting them. The more painful those failures are, the more the unhealthy enthusiasts tend to turn the other way. When realizing any mistake, they naturally reframe and move on. What this means is that they will cast a positive light or attribute the error to external factors along the following lines:

» "It was not meant to be; I will have better luck the next time."

» "The founder was deceitful; everyone else got duped."

» "Markets are bad now, but it will return; fundamentals remain intact. Nothing wrong with my investment thesis."

Unhealthy Type Sevens are less likely to introspect and determine what went wrong with their original investment decisions. To do so may invite pain, which must be avoided. Why marinate in thoughts of inadequacies or shortcomings when a Type Seven investor can find a ready excuse to explain the mistake away without self-reproach? Therein lies the rub: The more pain is avoided, the less likely one can develop into a better investor. The price of failure escalates by omission of personal responsibility because repeating that failure becomes more likely.

In contrast, mindful Type Sevens conduct proper postmortems with the same gumption as they chase their futures. They comb through the wreckage to find causes, enduring the discomfort of painful truths because it is therapeutic. By daring to look backward and inward, these Type Seven investors become wiser.

ROAD MAP
FOR TYPE SEVEN INVESTORS

How do you work with the personality of "I Want It All" Sevens? Telling a Type Seven to put aside a chunk of salary each month into a traditional savings account is like telling Nicki Minaj not to bare her behind on Instagram. Even if you can rein in Type Sevens through overt restrictions, it will not last. Just like Nicki Minaj, who quit Instagram in November 2019 only to post again in January 2020, Type Sevens —and Nicki's behind—are unstoppable. This calls for a balanced approach that aligns with their experience-driven personalities without making them feel deprived of opportunities.

HOMEOWNERSHIP AS AN ANCHORING EXPERIENCE

If Type Sevens aim for homeownership as their first investment and save up for the down payment, that process may prove foundational to early financial hygiene. Paying down a thirty-year mortgage is a practical forcing function to build equity and funnel money away from impulsive spending or big bets.

Type Seven investors should visualize the joys of homeownership: becoming masters of their own domains and being freed from the limitations of living in rented spaces. The potential pain of fiscal restraint can then be reframed as a worthy sacrifice.

The choice of homes is an important decision, and it cannot be hasty, even if the enthusiast wants to move fast. Guardrails must be observed to prevent them from buying castles they cannot afford. Working with the right agents or advisers can make a difference. Nicholas Cage famously sued his accountant for negligence after reportedly overspending on countless purchases, including two European castles.

DIVERSIFICATION AS A HEDGE

At some point, Type Sevens will come across investment ideas that fire up their imaginations. Relentless curiosity and networking almost always lead to such opportunities. Some of the most successful companies in recent history, such as Spotify, Boston Dynamics, and SpaceX, are examples of wild concepts brought to life, rewarding early shareholders in the process.

When Type Sevens want to invest in the next big thing, "no" is unlikely to be acceptable, even if it originates from trusted advisers. More palatable is ensuring that any such investment is counterbalanced by an equal outlay in something less exciting, like a diversified exchange-traded fund, fixed-income instruments, or even gold. This will ensure sufficient diversification, effectively placing a cumulative cap on capital deployed into risky assets. We do not know what we do not know, and diversification is the best mitigation without imposing prohibition.

APPLY FIRST-PRINCIPLES THINKING

In multiple press interviews, Elon Musk has outlined his scientific approach to solving complex problems by referring to first-principles thinking. While he is controversial, few can dispute his technical mind, which has led to groundbreaking innovations across multiple industries.

First-principles thinking is an antithesis to reasoning by analogy; it challenges hidden assumptions and questions logical extrapolations that may be flawed. But the approach is nothing new. It is often known as out-of-the-box or independent thinking. The below quote from a 2017 *Rolling Stone* interview with Musk elucidates the first-principles method and how it may apply to Type Seven investors:

> **"I think it is important to reason from first principles rather than by analogy. So, the normal way we conduct our lives is, we reason by analogy. We are doing this because it is like something else that was done, or it is like what other people are doing, with slight iterations on a theme. And it is mentally easier to reason by analogy rather than from first principles. First principles [thinking] is kind of a physics way of looking at the world, and what that really means is, you boil things down to the most fundamental truths and say, "Okay, what are we sure is true?" and then reason up from there. That takes a lot more mental energy."**

Type Seven investors, though quick thinkers, tend to make mental leaps led by optimism, instant expertise, and expeditiousness. Saving mental energy by bypassing due process may lead to rash decisions. Accordingly, just being aware of Type Seven mental inclinations and the merits of a first-principles thinking process can help shine a spotlight on potential blind spots.

FORM AN A-TEAM TO STRENGTHEN INVESTMENT PROCESSES

The investing journey is more enjoyable for Type Sevens when others are involved since they are social animals and enjoy buoyant esprit de corps. Investment plans can become much more robust when they include diverse perspectives, similar to how Freddie Mercury produced some of his best music while working with his band Queen. Type Seven investors need to find their versions of Brian May, John Deacon, and Roger Taylor.

It is noted that none of those band members are anything like Freddie Mercury—each held his own. Type Seven investors will find the best collaborators in personalities who are most unlike them: individuals who are more conservative, disciplined, contemplative, and restrained. Ironically, these are also the kinds of people who are most likely to frustrate Type Sevens. To bridge the divide, potential collaborators must possess a more significant or different knowledge base stimulating enough for Type Seven investors to accept and respect their differences.

NO LEVERAGED TRADES

Type Sevens must not borrow to fund their portfolio when investing. They should avoid margin loans, options trading, and any leveraged instruments. More importantly, Type Sevens must not take personal loans, borrow from credit cards, or remortgage homes to invest. Given their rose-tinted lenses and tendency to overestimate their expertise, taking leverage is like amping adrenaline junkies up on steroids, further obscuring their clarity of mind. There is a quote from economist John Maynard Keynes: "Markets can stay irrational longer than investors can remain solvent." Personal investing is a lifelong journey, and we survive for the long haul by remaining liquid. Being forced to fold at the worst possible time could wipe one out for good.

DEVELOPMENT PLAN FOR SEVENS: INTEGRATING TOWARD TYPE FIVE (INVESTIGATOR) AND TYPE ONE (PERFECTIONIST)

In 1995, Elon Musk cofounded his first enterprise, Zip2, a provider and licensor of online city guide software to newspapers. It was sold to Compaq Computer within four years for $305 million, netting him a personal windfall of $22 million at the age of twenty-seven. Instead of taking a break, Musk jumped straight into the financial sector with his next venture: X.com. Even before his deal with Compaq Computer was consummated, Musk was already in the planning stages to disrupt traditional banking. His idea was to establish a wholly online bank—revolutionary in the late 1990s—to provide customers with a full suite of products, from checking and savings accounts to brokerages and insurance policies. Musk invested $12 million of his own money in X.com, an unusual move considering how easy it would have been for him to raise external funding in the wake of Zip2's success.

Musk, however, is a Type Seven archetype, and his entrepreneurial actions are nothing if not daring, precocious, and two steps ahead of everyone else. X.com would eventually merge with Peter Theil's Confinity to form PayPal, which was sold to eBay in 2002 for $1.5 billion. Subsequently, Musk parlayed his growing fortune to even greater heights, cofounding additional groundbreaking enterprises, including SpaceX, Tesla, Neuralink, and OpenAI. As if he did not have enough on his plate, Musk also bought out Twitter in 2022.

There is seemingly no end to Musk's ambition. Never has there been a business figure who defies all conventional wisdom of scope. From financial technology and social media to electric vehicles and rocket science, Musk is almost limitless in what he can accomplish. He is famously hands-on and detail-oriented and does not simply seed businesses with money to realize his visions. At Tesla, this multibillionaire would sleep on factory floors alongside engineers and operational crew to solve daily production issues when scaling Model 3 proved to be his greatest career challenge. When Musk became interested in space technology, he imbibed college textbooks on rocketry and propulsion, dedicating himself to learning everything about the topic; in the process, Musk saw the potential in building reusable rockets and subsequently formed SpaceX.

In Enneagram speak, Musk is a Type Seven who has fully integrated into the hardcore habits of Type One perfectionists and the intellectual self-reliance of Type Five investigators. His combination of imaginativeness, self-conviction, grit, and mastery over multiple disciplines has made him one of the greatest inventors of the twenty-first century. With pun intended, Musk is a Model 7.

Looking at Musk, it is evident that the pivots Type Sevens need to make in their development paths are in the direction of Type One (perfectionist) and Type Five (investigator). Both represent counterbalancing traits to the urgent energies of an enthusiast.

Leaning into the meticulousness of a Type One perfectionist can lend structure and focus to the excitable Type Sevens, who may jump from one rabbit hole to another if they are not conscientious. In times of difficulties and obstacles, the best Type Ones are pragmatic and persevere through their commitments with self-discipline. Assuming these qualities will counteract tendencies to ignore details and escape pain.

Likewise, borrowing from the Type Five playbook can inspire Type Sevens to incorporate stillness into their nervous systems. Being in perpetual motion may not achieve results, and jumping straight into trial and error can be damaging. Taking mindful moments to contemplate like an investigator—versus allowing the monkey mind to drive the bus—can mold enthusiasts into more strategic thinkers.

Taking a step back, more complicated personal development for these outgoing personalities may involve analyzing their inner worlds by looking back further than they are used to. What deeper pains could they be harboring? We all have specific memories from childhood and adolescence that we must come to terms with. Escapism may be how Type Seven learned to engage with reality in their younger days. There may be an amorphous and unrelenting void that many Type Sevens are trying hard to fill with their unquenchable thirst for everything, from creation and consumption to risk-taking. Until that void can be identified and reconciled, escape hatches will be relied upon. To be complete and whole, acceptance is essential. Harnessing some of those energies inward to investigate one's inner world may be worth more than a thousand adventures.

The process of personal investing can be revealing. Healthy Type Sevens exercise discernment in making portfolio moves, neither hurried nor avaricious in their risk appetite. Money on its own may not mean as much to a balanced Type Seven, who is living in the present rather than fixating on an abundant life in the future. They document deliberations, study details, and accept their mistakes as they surface. The best Type Seven investors retain their unique characteristics of being intellectually curious, positive, and likable. When Type Sevens see themselves slowing down to be more contemplative, this suggests that their inner pain is well into the process of dissolving.

Chapter 10

Type Eight:
Daenerys Targaryen (of *Game of Thrones*)

I remember watching the final episode of *Game of Thrones* (2011–2019) and my shock when Jon Snow plunged his dagger into Daenerys Targaryen. How could he? How dare he! I had been rooting for her to ascend the Iron Throne for almost eight seasons! She was Daenerys Stormborn of House Targaryen, "rightful heir to the Iron Throne, rightful Queen of the Andals and the First Men, Protector of the Seven Kingdoms, Mother of Dragons, the Khaleesi of the Great Grass Sea, the Unburnt, the Breaker of Chains!"

My first reaction was that the showrunners had cheated me out of the returns on my emotional investment. Throughout the series—except for the last couple of episodes—Daenerys Targaryen is positioned as one of the main contenders for the role of the "Prince That Was Promised," on an epic hero's journey. Beginning as a powerless underdog abused by her brother, this Breaker of Chains matures and grows in strength to become an awe-inspiring ruler, outsmarting wicked men and winning loyal followers across Essos. She accumulates more ships than Mærsk and frees countless slaves, like some medieval Harriet Tubman. From start to finish, she looks flawless in haute couture. This dragon lady is the kind of leader we dream about: compassionate, heroic, wise, and photogenic. Until the show takes a dark turn. Suddenly, she is a female Joseph Stalin.

In hindsight, her character arc from goddess to destroyer is not as unbelievable and off-the-wall as disgruntled *Game of Thrones* fans might claim. For a Type Eight (challenger) personality, creation and destruction are two sides of the same coin; both originate from the same impulses. Daenerys Targaryen merely flips from one to the other when her world crumbles.

For eight seasons, this pivotal character embodies the full spectrum of a Type Eight personality, also known as a "leader" in the Enneagram world. At her best, she is a resourceful leader, courageous yet patient, commanding and magnanimous at the same time. She inspires great men like Tyrion Lannister, Ser Jorah Mormont, and Ser Barristan Selmy to pledge allegiance and support her claim to the Iron Throne. Even Jon Snow, ever stoic, falls in love with her greatness. Such is the power of Type Eights at their peak. They are irresistible.

However, the ego fixation of this Enneagram type is on vengeance, and it always lurks somewhere in the psyche, even in the minds of healthy Type Eights. In the last season, cracks appear as Daenerys wages war against Cersei Lannister. Losing two of her three dragons (she refers to them as her children) marks the beginning of the end, as they represent a crucial source of protection and power. The sudden demise of her trusted counselors (and friends) Missandei and Ser Jorah Mormont removes emotional support and voices of reason. A weakened claim on the Iron Throne, when Jon Snow's true parentage is revealed, makes Daenerys feel even more disempowered. Worst of all, Jon Snow withdraws his affection when he realizes their blood relation. All these things combine to set the stage for an unhealthy Type Eight to emerge.

Revenge now moves front and center: She annihilates King's Landing in the name of liberation. With her sights set further, Daenerys Targaryen vows to continue her crusade regardless of the human cost. Gone is her compassion, replaced by ruthlessness and coldhearted ambition. She devolves into a cruel dictator, declaring what is good for the world, and is no longer open to counsel. In other words, she is now the Mad Queen, and destruction is her answer to everything.

Death is inevitable for this Type Eight gone mad as a hatter.

PERSONALITY OF TYPE EIGHTS (CHALLENGERS)

Type Eights are typified by their quest for power. Their mannerisms tend to be assertive, direct, and urgent. They take up space and radiate energy. For visual cues, picture the personalities of popular alpha leaders we know: Martin Luther King Jr., Winston Churchill, and Thanos, the Marvel supervillain who is hell-bent on accessorizing himself with Infinity Stones to reset the universe.

Of all Enneagram types, Type Eight may be the easiest to spot since they literally stand out from the pack. These natural-born leaders are motivated by their need to be stronger than others because this is how they have learned to survive and protect themselves since they were young. They are independent and like to minimize reliance on anyone. When taken to extremes, Type Eights may downplay their emotional needs and focus instead on their worldly goals. They are reluctant to be vulnerable because they fear people disappointing or taking advantage of them. They repress softer emotions like sadness, loneliness, fear, guilt, and shame. Anger reigns.

Type Eights quickly accept challenges of any kind if doing so will demonstrate strength to themselves and others. They enjoy feeling triumphant when overcoming the odds to emerge victorious. Strong willpower, endurance, and persistence are primary qualities of Type Eights; neither hesitation nor subtlety suits them, as either could signal feebleness. These conquerors act on gut instinct and are quick to respond with boldness. There is little room for self-doubt or inhibiting concerns over how they might appear to others in their quest for greatness.

Professionally, they tend to be larger than life. Many become entrepreneurs as they prefer to take charge. Those seeking employment strive to climb the corporate ladder and typically succeed because of their can-do spirit. A healthy Type Eight boss is an exemplary champion of good causes—the kind people want in their corners to fight for their next promotions. As team players, however, Type Eights may fall short as their preference is always to do it their way.

In a social setting, Type Eights tend to be extroverted. They are vibrant and confident, and many can be boastful in their actions, from being the best dressed to driving the nicest cars in the neighborhood. You either love or hate them, but you cannot ignore them. They pride themselves on being straight talkers; in other words, they do not have the filters most people possess. Conversations with Type Eights can get heated since they do not shy away from confrontation. To them, uncensored exchanges build connections, although others may feel quite the opposite.

A healthy Type Eight is someone like Daenerys Targaryen before she starts unraveling. She tempers personal ambitions with compassion and pursues causes greater than herself. Self-belief is balanced by a keen awareness of one's limitations and the need to enlist others to accomplish lofty ambitions. The best Type Eight leaders empower others with trust and open minds, collaborating rather than dictating. No coercion or threat is necessary to pursue their goals since they inspire devotees to join their causes instead of ruling by fiat. Healthy Type Eights do not come across as willful or egocentric since they are not threatened by others or fearful of sharing power. Their strength and courage elicit deep respect as they seek to remake the environment for the greater good. As friends, healthy Eights are warm, protective, and generous.

Unhealthy Type Eights are your worst nightmare, the kind of megalomaniacs who wage wars against anyone obstructing their paths. Perceiving the world as a battleground, their solution is to exert as much external control as possible to achieve victory and keep themselves safe.

Intimidation is a modus operandi employed by these tyrants without any moral or ethical compass for self-awareness. When the world does not conform to their narrow visions, their willingness to destroy others (and even themselves) makes them dangerous personalities.

CHECKLIST FOR TYPE EIGHT

If you respond "Yes" to, or resonate with, most of the questions and the statements below, you are likely to be a Type Eight:

- ☐ You pride yourself on being a straight talker and want others to be the same.
- ☐ Coming across as too intense or ambitious to others as you pursue your objectives does not concern you.
- ☐ You tend to make decisions quickly based on gut instincts.
- ☐ Growing up, you had ambivalent relationships with your parents or caregivers. You often needed to toughen up and rely more on yourself than them.
- ☐ You are fearless against bullies and have a history of standing up against them, even if they are in positions of power over you (parents, teachers, bosses).
- ☐ You enjoy taking on complex challenges to push yourself and feel triumphant whenever you beat the odds.
- ☐ At work, you do not shy away from confrontation, even with your bosses.
- ☐ You constantly assess your superiors or anyone with authority—including government figures and heads of organizations to which you belong—to judge their leadership skills, especially regarding whether they are strong or weak.

☐ You embrace "Go big or go home" as a life philosophy.
☐ You are not afraid to take charge at work and in social settings.

TYPE EIGHT INVESTORS

Amid all that plotting and scheming to get on top, one wonders if Type Eights even have time for mundane financial planning. Are they better off raising proverbial armies and dragons to seize power and multiply their armada? I do not recall Daenerys Targaryen ever discussing investment opportunities with her master of coin (does she even have one?) on the show.

To Type Eights, money is power and a means to an end. Having abundant resources means not having to rely on or submit to anyone for a living. Type Eight investors are perhaps the gutsiest Enneagram archetype in the gut triad. Absent the compulsion to follow rules like Type One perfectionists or the hesitation to engage in conflict like Type Nine peacemakers, these challenger types—unlike their instinctual counterparts—are always ready to pounce.

In the hands of healthy Type Eights, money is a means to champion people and build purposeful enterprises. On the other end of the spectrum, unhealthy Eights may view money more as a tool to assert authority over others. To them, it is not enough to attain financial independence. Only having vast resources will ensure their ruling status.

CORE MOTIVATION: TO BE IN CONTROL IN DECISION-MAKING

Having the agency to make independent decisions is paramount to Type Eights. These leaders want to be in charge of money, whether in the form of saving, spending, investing, or donating. They may or may not be qualified to make certain choices, but that is beside the point. So long as they are the boss, other considerations are secondary. And they will stick to their decisions. Consequently, contrarian advice may be viewed as an attempt to overrule them unless it comes from sources the Type Eight investor respects.

This has multiple implications for their personal investing journeys. When well informed and objective, Type Eight investors can be steadfast in their convictions and make investments based on merits while not conforming to the mainstream. They may be among the first to identify disruptive technologies and take early positions in verticals like electric vehicles, e-commerce platforms, fintech, and cloud computing. On the other hand, unhealthy Type Eight investors can be obstinate in their views and refuse to consider external opinions, regardless of merits.

PRIMARY INFATUATION: GO BIG OR GO HOME

With intense energy, Type Eight investors love big ideas and making significant investments. Taking concentrated risks aligns with their bravado and self-belief. In some cases, where they have meaningful stakes and can even exercise control over management teams, feelings of importance and centrality are heightened. In contrast, diversification may connote feebleness and indecisiveness, traits Type Eights detest and avoid.

When left unchecked, Type Eight investors tend to act quickly on instinct, craving alpha returns to match their alpha mindset. Challengers are liable to make impulsive investments or purchase palatial homes that are unaffordable or overpriced. They may unthinkingly favor investments that offer manifold potential upsides over bland blue-chip enterprises or vanilla-but-reliable investments like fixed income, cash savings, and index funds. Type Eight investors may also invest in high-risk, early-stage companies for reasons that relate more to their egos than objectivity.

A concentrated and risky portfolio is likely when one is free of self-doubt.

KEY AVOIDANCE: ADMITTING AND REVIEWING MISTAKES

Given Type Eight investors' intent on making and living consequential decisions, they tend to avoid situations that stir up vulnerabilities. Nothing evokes the soft underbellies of emotion like confronting one's own mistakes. Some people will wallow in self-blame—think Type Four individualists—and some put on their thinking hats to perform anxious postmortems, like Type Six skeptics. For Type Eights who lack self-restraint and self-awareness, anger is a go-to response to any missteps they make on their financial journeys. They may look for scapegoats to protect their egos and avoid feeling responsible.

Type Eights may also recoil from looking backward or inward. They just want to keep moving forward. For that reason, investment mistakes may be swept under the carpet and denied, lest Eights feel powerless in the face of losses. The price of doing so may be the forgoing of invaluable lessons that can be mined from blunders, whether due to external factors or one's own doing.

CHIEF PROVOCATION: LOSING CONTROL

There is no certainty about how Mr. Market will grade our investments in the future. Surefire winners can turn into outright disasters, as did retail giants Sears and Abercrombie & Fitch, once favored by many investors. Some come back from the dead or rise from the ashes: Think Microsoft when cloud computing jolted its flaccid growth and Salesforce when it was the first software-as-a-service company to go public in the wake of the dot-com crash.

With so much unknown, investing is risky, and black swan events can take a toll on anyone. This unpredictability does not sit well with Type Eights and their intense need for control over the external environment.

BLIND SPOT #1: ANYTHING BETWEEN BLACK AND WHITE

Decisions based on instincts are usually fast and almost reflexive. Intuition plays a leading role here, and Type Eight investors tend to see things in stark contrasts: winners versus losers, market disruptors versus doomed failures, industry visionaries versus incompetent leaders. No room for shades of gray in between. They may view a company as either the next Amazon or the next GoPro. Taking a nuanced view is not their strength. Since rationale counts less in forming their opinions, it is also hard for Type Eight investors to see alternative perspectives. Their confidence—justified or not—hinders them from questioning their investment theses.

The quality of decisions will hence depend on who is making the call. An experienced and grounded Type Eight investor can be astute, separating winners from losers without getting lost in the weeds. On the other side, someone acting on their gut without the requisite expertise is flying blind.

BLIND SPOT #2: MAKING A POINT IS NOT EVERYTHING

Type Eights enjoy their confrontations and love to make dramatic statements. They often talk more and listen less to what others are saying. When it comes to investing, it is helpful to at least pay attention to contrasting schools of thinking. Except for saving bonds or very low-risk fixed-income instruments, investment opportunities are seldom as they appear on the surface. Since we do not know what we do not know, having a broader view of differing angles from multiple sources (provided they are credible) is essential to forming a more balanced thesis.

Teasing out questions to prod one's conviction creates more robust investment cases. Headstrong Type Eight investors, though, may get defensive and misinterpret opposing arguments as a contest of wills. Getting into a debate with unhealthy Type Eights is intimidating and pointless since they tend to argue less on facts than on pride. Relationships—whether professional or personal—can turn adversarial as a result. People who experience feisty Type Eights in disagreements may start to distance themselves, leaving them disgusted and covered in bruises.

TYPE EIGHTS: WHEN DEALING WITH INVESTMENT SUCCESSES AND FAILURES

Type Eight investors have the guts to take asymmetrical investment risks for financial and psychological rewards. Even if collective wisdom points in the other direction, Type Eight investors are not afraid to take a stand and vote with their capital. They can feel even more invincible when they hit home runs on their investments.

Type Eight investors will typically discount any randomness that might have contributed to their successes. Everything happens because of their ingenuity and daring. In cases where other individuals were involved in making those investments, unhealthy Type Eight investors might take more than their fair share of credit and pat themselves on the back for picking the right coconspirators. Their lack of self-awareness or humility may lead to larger investment risks, potentially putting their financial security on the line. On the other hand, healthy Type Eight investors, though still possessing an appetite for risks, remain grounded and know their limitations. They are not foolhardy, and they acknowledge the perpetual roles that luck (and black swans) plays in life and investing.

What happens when investments go awry? As investors, we have no control over eventual outcomes. Even fixed-income instruments come with default risks, and rock-solid property investments can underperform for various reasons. Market forces can deviate from fundamentals within a short time frame and create price turbulence. To Type Eight investors who like to stay in control, being subject to the whims of market swings can incite visceral frustration. Markets are an affront to their fundamental need to control everything and everyone.

Yet adversity is familiar territory for Type Eights, and overcoming challenges to return stronger is their forte. Those with sufficient self-restraint and awareness will regroup to assess the situation before deciding whether any actions need to be taken. Unhealthy Type Eight investors who are missing a pause button may shoot from the hip (or, more specifically, the gut) to reassert control. Overreaction is a common error in a volatile market, but many Type Eights cannot help themselves, especially when feeling blindsided. Doing nothing is not an option when their fight-or-flight instincts are triggered. This increases the risk of making irreversible mistakes.

ROAD MAP FOR TYPE EIGHT INVESTORS

With intense energy and an instinct to act, the challenge for Type Eight is to do less, not more. Audacity may feel empowering, but when it comes to personal investing, there is no need for nonstop action like in a *Mission Impossible* movie. As Warren Buffett has pointed out, the great baseball slugger Ted Williams said he hit so many home runs because of all the bad pitches he did not swing at.

A common investment strategy that Type Eights employ is hiring external parties to manage their financial affairs. While it may seem like relinquishing control, Type Eight investors view finding accountable people to manage and grow their financial resources to be more like delegation. Such professional help can be a traditional financial adviser with discretionary powers or a property agent fielding real estate deals. Selecting and managing relationships with the right advisers is vital to successful collaborations. If Type Eight investors give in to their habitual distrust and domineering ways and override critical decisions themselves, they will negate the benefits of outside counsel.

FIND COLLABORATORS AND MAINTAIN INTERACTIVE RELATIONSHIPS

Most people do not assert their thoughts and ideas with the same vigor and force as Type Eights. In the presence of these alpha species, they may end up speaking less. Worse, they get blown out of the room.

Type Eight investors need to be aware of their potential impact—intentional or not—on others, ensuring they do not dominate discussions and neutralize the checks and balances that others can offer. Type Eight investors should lean more into listening and recognize that acknowledging (not necessarily agreeing with) alternative perspectives is not disempowering but quite the opposite. Maintaining healthy, functional relationships with collaborators is paramount; care must be taken to observe boundaries and professionalism. Not everyone needs to respond quickly or decisively. Type Eights, with their tendency to anticipate rejection and betrayal, should be mindful of how biases can influence their perceptions of people. When subject to excessive Type Eight intensity, relationships can quickly turn tenuous.

A word of caution: Type Eights should not hire friends in any role involving money. Temperatures rise fast on financial matters, so it is best to protect personal relationships from contentious situations.

HOMEOWNERSHIP: LORD OF ONE'S DOMAIN

The idea of being lorded over by a landlord contradicts Type

Eight's affinity for self-governance. Hence, homeownership should be prioritized early on their investing journeys. Buying a property is generally a sound financial investment if proper due diligence is carried out and one is not overpaying. However, the risk unique to Type Eight investors is biting off more than they can chew. A swaggering home may show importance, but Type Eights need to check their egos at the door to prevent overstretching financial means that can lead to costly consequences.

DIVERSIFICATION AS A DEFENSE AGAINST SELF

Portfolio diversification is not to be confused with indecisiveness or cowardice. As much as Type Eights believe in their abilities, diversification should be seen as a means of protecting their assets from the unknown. Even the most established companies and asset classes have seen tides turn against them: Enron, BlackBerry, Bear Stearns, Nokia, office properties in the world of hybrid work, and centuries-old commodities like coal. With technology, no investment is immutable. Accordingly, diversification is essential, even for these intrepid investors.

Much of their portfolio should combine lower-risk assets such as lower-risk exchange-traded funds, home equity, diversified real estate, fixed income, cash, large capitalization stocks, and perhaps gold. No single-name investment should constitute more than 2.5 percent of the portfolio (based on capital deployed), no matter how confident a Type Eight investor may feel. Diversification across a wide range of industry sectors is also recommended.

AVOID LEVERAGE AND ALL-IN BETS

Like Type Seven investors, Type Eights have the urge to go big on everything. Limiting risk exposure so that no mistake turns fatal is an essential guardrail. Leverage, except home mortgages, must be avoided; the same applies to any risk-taking that may result in sudden and disproportionate losses arising from volatility. Because many Type Eight investors may struggle to distinguish between objective confidence and egocentricity, all-in bets should never be made.

PAUSE BEFORE TAKING INVESTMENT ACTIONS

Driven to exert control through gut instinct, Type Eight investors are used to swift actions and reactions. But in making major decisions like buying a house, the devil is often in the details. A practical forcing function to pause is to require cross-checks with external parties. Getting second opinions that do not come from yes-men is imperative: The goal is to seek effective sounding boards, not echo chambers.

BEWARE OF EXCESSES

Frugality may be a foreign concept to many Type Eights, but self-restraint in fiscal matters is an essential building block to attaining financial freedom. With a strong inclination to be bombastic, Type Eights should exercise intentional mindfulness with their spending. Are they buying something ostentatious? Can they afford it? These are some questions that Type Eights should ask themselves when making significant purchases. Luxury companies hone their marketing messages to resonate with our most impulsive desires. Sports cars with formidable speeds, leather goods that signify a swaggering personal aura, and prestigious club memberships that elicit envy—these are designed to appeal to those who crave power and importance.

DEVELOPMENT PLAN FOR EIGHTS: INTEGRATING TOWARD TYPE TWO (GIVER) AND TYPE FIVE (INVESTIGATOR)

> "Man must evolve for all human conflict a method which rejects revenge, aggression, and retaliation. The foundation of such a method is love."
>
> *Martin Luther King Jr.*

The book *Fooled by Randomness* by Nassim Nicholas Taleb discusses human limitations and our tendency to see causality where there is none. As much as we like to believe we can control everything in life by pulling the right levers, and none more so than Type Eights, the world is far more complicated. A higher power rules, and it is called randomness. This may grate every fiber of a Type Eight's being, but it is a powerful truth that must be acknowledged. Randomness is far more pervasive and influential than we want to believe, given how much the human mind desires to rationalize everything into equations of inputs and outputs.

The primary fear of Type Eights is being harmed or controlled by others. Growing up, they are likely to have felt disconnected from their parents in some profound way that hardened their personality. Without feeling sufficiently protected or nurtured, they develop an early need to be strong, whether it is to defend themselves or others in the family. Internal strength swells in tandem with external distrust as these young challengers increasingly believe in self-reliance. They need to be in charge to feel safe and keep those feelings of abandonment or rejection at bay. As courageous as Type Eights may be, their bluster conceals a genuine fear of recognizing their vulnerabilities. Admitting human weaknesses means feeling less able to cope in a world perceived as hostile during childhood. For this reason, Type Eights tend to reject randomness as a concept since the unknown threatens their sense of safety.

In the last episode of *Game of Thrones*, Daenerys Targaryen becomes queen of the Seven Kingdoms after destroying King's Landing. Yet Jon Snow kills her with a simple dagger. No elaborate ruse or weaponry is needed to carry out the assassination. Even the most powerful dragon by her side and an army at her command cannot keep her safe. Her death is a black swan event that she could not have anticipated or prevented. She instigates the realization of her deepest fear when she strikes King's Landing with a force that matches her towering rage. Her quest for limitless power proves to be her undoing.

Like Daenerys Targaryen, Type Eight investors can amass all the financial might in the world, but absent self-restraint, an aggressive appetite for risk can be self-destructive. Remote but dire consequences can take them miles back on their financial journeys. When that happens, they are blindsided. This underscores the need for Type Eight investors to establish strict guardrails, to protect not against others but against their overdoing.

As much as Type Eights do not like to ponder a power more significant than the self, the universe is full of randomness beyond our comprehension or control. This does not suggest we should not strive hard for success but rather acknowledges that outcomes can still be unexpected regardless of processes and efforts exerted. Rather than being so focused on results, Type Eights need to make an allowance for their vulnerabilities and curveballs. No one is spared from randomness—not even the most powerful of all Enneagram types.

For Type Eights prone to distrust, money may seem like the only dependable resource, but it is no substitute for genuine human relationships. Love is not a distraction, and receiving affection does not weaken Type Eights. Taking on a Type Two (giver) role will help bring back the emotional growth truncated while growing up. The world is more than just a place to be conquered; it can also be full of joyful surprises. Learning to love others truly will restore a Type Eight's faith in the universe and bring balance to ambitions rooted in fear of being harmed. Reestablishing the trust and innocence lost in childhood by loving others is critical to personal development.

Another transformative pivot for Type Eights is to assume the quiet, contemplative style of a Type Five specialist. Reining in their external energy to refocus on purposeful deliberation can help Type Eights master self-control and counterbalance their outward tendencies. This restraint also mitigates the odds of knee-jerk reactions that may prove unwise, especially when making major decisions.

Type Eights must appreciate that not everything needs to be controlled for happiness to transpire. When they ease back into themselves and recognize their human limitations, they will expend less energy trying to fight the odds all the time. Instead, they can rediscover the happiness (and love) of connecting with oneself and others. That will make their personal investing journeys and lives much easier and less strenuous.

Chapter 11

Type Nine:
Annie MacDuggan (of *The First Wives Club*)

When *The First Wives Club* was released in 1996, it was not expected to do well. The film focuses on three middle-aged divorcées—each a first wife—seeking revenge against their ex-husbands who left them for younger women. Commercial expectations were low, even though the cast was top-notch (Bette Midler! Goldie Hawn! Diane Keaton! Maggie Smith! "Showgirl" Elizabeth Berkley!) and the movie was backed by a major studio. Critics did not like it. Perhaps most of the reviewers were men, and they were turned off by a script that aimed to castrate (metaphorically) all the primary male characters.

Against all odds, *The First Wives Club* was a smash. It opened atop the box office with $18.9 million, outgrossing testosterone-filled (and higher budgeted) *Last Man Standing* by more than two to one. The three leads (Midler, Hawn, Keaton) even appeared on the cover of *Time* magazine following the film's success. *The First Wives Club* became a cultural phenomenon and the tenth-highest-grossing movie in the US that year. In other words, people loved it. Something about the movie resonated: The storyline about finding renewed meaning in life outside of failed marriages must have struck a chord with the audience. Beneath the media sensation, it is a heartfelt human tale about overcoming individual setbacks to find self-empowerment.

Of the three main characters, Annie MacDuggan (played by Keaton) has the most dramatic story arc. At first, MacDuggan comes across as calm and cheerful, even after admitting to being separated from her husband of twenty-five years. She carries herself with an unconvincing optimism that appears so disconnected from reality that her friends think she is taking lithium, a mood stabilizer.

That might as well be the case. By insisting that everything is just fine, MacDuggan lives in a state of dissociation, which numbs her true thoughts and feelings. She continues to idealize her husband and pines for reconciliation. Even her own daughter calls her a doormat. As her therapist points out, MacDuggan has a problem with anger. It is there but repressed because she does not wish to risk her relationships. Her peace of mind is held together by the roles she plays, especially that of a wife. Admitting to a broken marriage and acknowledging who her husband really is as a person would have been too much. Self-denial becomes an easy drug for MacDuggan.

Soon, things come to a head. Her husband asks for a divorce—postcoital—and MacDuggan finds out that he is getting married to their marriage therapist. At this point, there is no more hiding, and her anger is unleashed in epic proportions.

This marks the beginning of MacDuggan's path toward independence. Ironically, the outcome she fears most—divorce—happens to be the wake-up call she needs. She forms a groundbreaking women's center with the other two ex-wives and resumes her career. When her ex-husband asks for a reconciliation, MacDuggan tells him to drop dead.

Annie MacDuggan is a prime example of a Type Nine (peacemaker) and goes through the entire process of disintegration and reintegration in 103 minutes. By the film's end, she is at her finest: self-assured, decisive, and authentic. By rejecting her ex-husband and seeing through him, MacDuggan honors her instincts. No longer avoiding reality or fearing separation, she embraces changes in her life and unleashes her inner Rambo, as her therapist puts it.

PERSONALITY OF TYPE NINES
(PEACEMAKERS)

Type Nine personalities are warm and welcoming, defined by their deep desire for harmony with people and the environment. Getting into repeated conflicts to get what they want is not their modus operandi. Peacemakers prefer mixing positivity with diplomacy. Some of the most beloved leaders are purported to be Type Nines, including Barack Obama, Bill Clinton, and Walt Disney.

Alongside Type Ones (perfectionists) and Type Eights (challengers), Type Nines belong to the instinctive triad. While Type One perfectionists project their instincts inward to become idealized versions of themselves and Type Eight challengers direct energies outward to control externalities, Type Nines employ a mixed approach. To maintain their inner Zen, they work on managing both external and internal dissonances.

Healthy Type Nines may not be the first to start a fight, but they are also not afraid to disturb the peace when aroused by their instinctual energies. Neither fearing repercussions on relationships nor subordinating themselves to others, these Type Nines are candid with their thoughts and feelings but always diplomatic. Because authentic relationships come with full acknowledgment of the good and bad, healthy Type Nines work through conflicts rather than avoiding them.

The best peacemakers accept their flaws, perceiving themselves with compassion and objectivity. By extension, they do the same for the people around them. Genuine empathy develops as they acknowledge shades of gray in everyone, and this helps them make sense of disparate viewpoints. They see people for who they are and intuit what others desire; hence, well-developed peacemakers are masterful negotiators. They are known to bridge irreconcilable differences and establish win-win scenarios.

On the other hand, unhealthy Type Nines prefer everything in soft focus. Rather than allowing reality into their psyche, they have built-in Instagram filters that gloss over painful truths. In the name of inner peace, conflicting thoughts and feelings are suppressed lest they trigger complex changes. Recall Annie MacDuggan of *The First Wives Club* and her initial Pollyannaish attitude toward her failing marriage, cheating husband, controlling mother, and low self-esteem. Problems are ignored and swept under the carpet, with nothing ugly left in plain sight.

Unhealthy peacemakers resist reality and pay a high personal price, often their self-respect. By turning a blind eye to disconcertment, they lose touch with themselves and develop a deep sense of unworthiness, further deadening their natural instincts. Therein lies the perpetual three-way tension between their compulsion to go along with others in harmony, unconscious yearnings to express their free will, and fears of rocking the boat. Such struggles are exhausting, sapping away the energy to take corrective actions.

CHECKLIST FOR TYPE NINE

If you respond "Yes" to, or resonate with, most of the questions and the statements below, you are likely to be a Type Nine:

- ☐ The main reason to avoid conflict—or contain your anger toward others—is a fear of destroying relationships rather than maintaining a public image.
- ☐ You like to spend time attending activities that are routine and familiar because they feel comforting.
- ☐ The sayings "Go with the flow" and "Why rock the boat?" resonate with you.

- ☐ You embrace the peace of the status quo more than the highs of setting lofty goals or pursuing wildest dreams.
- ☐ You prefer to look on the bright side, abiding by words of wisdom—such as "Everything happens for a reason" and "Whatever will be, will be"—that have seen you through difficult times.
- ☐ Expressing your opinions openly is not something that you naturally do.
- ☐ When asked to make necessary or even urgent decisions, you tend to take your time because you do not like to feel hurried.
- ☐ You sometimes feel anger for not being able to draw clear boundaries with others.
- ☐ Even with a defined agenda list, you often get sidetracked by unexpected tasks that seem to pop up every time.
- ☐ "Easygoing" is a common term used to describe you; you feel a need to go along with everyone else, even when you disagree.

TYPE NINE INVESTORS

"You can't handle the truth."
A Few Good Men (1992)

A major challenge for Type Nine investors is facing the truth about their fiscal conditions and taking decisive action. There are a few requirements in life that one cannot escape, and money is one of them. Retirement planning is also something that cannot be put off for long—at least for most people—as there is a cost to prolonged inaction. Being oblivious to one's financial situation is not the same as having peace of mind. Deliberate avoidance to bypass exertion provides merely an illusion of calm.

Only when connected to the reality of fiscal needs, coupled with the implementation of action plans, will Type Nine investors attain the kind of inner stability they crave. Taking action need not entail immediate risk; it can begin with smaller steps in financial literacy, saving goals, and personal budgeting.

CORE MOTIVATION: TO MAINTAIN STATUS QUO

Change is difficult but an essential component of personal investing. As life progresses, financial needs evolve. Marriage, children, physical and mental health, and unexpected professional stumbles may require drastic pivots to meet new demands. The status quo only works for so long until it does not anymore. By that point, the challenge is to shift financial planning to fit new realities.

Where specific investments are concerned, few asset classes are immune to changing times. With technology upending almost all industries, fallen stars include the likes of JCPenney, Sears, Blockbuster, and Xerox. More companies from the current era will follow suit. Even currencies shift in relative strength, either over long periods—witness the gradual decline of the Great British pound—or with shocking suddenness, like the Indonesian rupiah during the 1997 Asian financial crisis and, more recently, the Venezuelan bolivar.

Holding on to the status quo may be a source of comfort because it is a known quantity, but it can be an expensive trap for Type Nine investors if they cling too tight. Change may feel threatening, but it is also inevitable.

PRIMARY INFATUATION: INNER PEACE

Having peace of mind when it comes to money is a tricky proposition. Nagging worries may be a sign that something is wrong and remedial actions must be taken before one can restore calmness. Or those worries could be irrational neuroses at work. Likewise, while not experiencing any worry at all may suggest mindfulness, contentment, and confidence in one's fiscal situation, it can also signify denial.

For Type Nine investors, inertia can feel like inner peace, even though it may result from fending off instincts in order to shield the psyche from upsetting truths. Delusion can persist until Type Nine investors experience rude wake-up calls.

KEY AVOIDANCE: TRUTH

Truth hurts. It is a common saying that resonates more as we develop better self-awareness. We all have coping mechanisms to manage realities. For Type Nine investors, their key coping mechanism is to tune reality out. Unhealthy peace-seeking investors numb their monetary concerns by focusing on the mundane or refusing to look at their finances. They may claim ignorance and over-rely on their spouses, families, or friends to make all the decisions. Ironically, when Type Nine investors avoid real-world deliberation to keep stress at bay, they may feel less at peace over time since staying in the background perpetuates an impression of invisibility, triggering Type Nines into bitter resentment.

CHIEF PROVOCATION: LACKING A SAY IN FINANCIAL MATTERS

Money touches almost every aspect of our lives, and we cannot ignore it. Even artists who say they care more about their art than money typically have business managers and accountants on their payroll to handle the numbers. The best creators are often shrewd businesspeople, retaining the ultimate say on major financial decisions.

Participating in monetary decisions that will determine our future is perhaps one of the most important concerns in life. Though Type Nine investors want to go with the flow and believe they are easygoing, their instincts may inform them otherwise. Bottling up contrarian opinions to keep the peace—with spouses, advisers, business partners, or families—can backfire because, deep down, Type Nines need to be seen and heard. Everyone does. They want to know that their thoughts, feelings, and instincts count, especially when making meaningful decisions. Merging with others at the expense of self-expression may buy some surface unity in the short run, but it will wind up sowing resentment deep in the Type Nine psyche.

BLIND SPOT #1: SELF-EFFICACY

When Type Nine investors take a far-too-passive approach to money matters, they miss out on learning more about the subject. A tendency to take the path of least resistance, partly due to a lack of self-confidence, may result in financial illiteracy. The more Type Nine investors give in to their passivity, the fewer opportunities they will have to exercise discretionary muscles in forging their financial paths. This can become a self-fulfilling prophecy, as hesitation feeds into more insecurity and inaction.

All personality types are equally qualified to handle personal investing. One does not need to be born with the organizational skills of a Type One perfectionist or possess the fearlessness of a Type Eight leader. Neither do we need to share common characteristics with famous fund managers or prominent financial gurus. Type Nine investors must not sacrifice self-development as they idealize others. They need to appreciate the power of their instinctive qualities to build themselves from the ground up. Forget self-effacement; Type Nines need to focus on self-efficacy.

BLIND SPOT #2: POWER TO SAY NO

It may be difficult for Type Nines to feel understood. After all, if they self-censor for fear of impacting relationships and merge with others to maintain cohesion, it becomes even more challenging for others to grasp who they are. People will assume these Type Nines to be more easygoing than they really are. Where personal investing is concerned, perhaps relevant parties—spouses, advisers, friends, families, partners—will end up making decisions on their behalf.

Therein lies the rub. The more Type Nines hold back, the more misunderstood they become, relegating themselves further to the background. Type Nine investors must believe they have just as much right to take up space because someone else will occupy theirs if they do not. Type Nines owe it to themselves to take discretionary action—and to say no when their rational instincts tell them so.

TYPE NINES:
WHEN DEALING WITH INVESTMENT
SUCCESSES AND FAILURES

Because retaining inner peace counts more for Type Nine investors than for any other Enneagram type, extreme highs and lows of personal investing are almost incongruent. Type Nine investors are more even-keeled than Type Eight investors who want to conquer alpha returns or Type Five investors who relish the intellectual game. This does not mean that all Type Nine investors will sit on cash, but they gravitate toward investment options that give them ease of mind, heart, and body. The best Type Nine investors devise portfolios that strike the right balance among risks, returns, and alignment of personal objectives.

Success for a Type Nine investor may be defined in multiple ways. If they have installed solid plans that evolve with changing circumstances and are confident they are not glossing over financial pain, this may be seen as a success. Owning their accomplishments, they may grow bolder and lean into a Type Three (performer) pivot to achieve more, while remaining relaxed within limits set by themselves, not others.

On the other hand, unhealthy Type Nine investors may ignore financial matters altogether, and if that gives them peace of mind, it is a success for them. Or they may allow others to deal with money, detaching themselves from arduous decision-making. That can be defined as success as well. While withdrawal and passivity may feel good in the short run, an objective reality check by time or third parties will often reveal the truth.

When an investment blows up, unhealthy coping mechanisms of disengagement and inaction may emerge. Losses and mistakes are downplayed because failures may be too difficult to absorb. Rather than leaning into problems, they may convince themselves that all will be well with unrealistic positivity. Refusal to respond in proportion to issues will impair good judgment over time. Unhealthy Type Nine investors may even resist all external help.

ROAD MAP
FOR TYPE NINE INVESTORS

Type Nines must believe they can become capable investors and must challenge themselves to be action-biased and purposeful. They may struggle at first, but once they lean into their Type One perfectionist wing to find rhythm, they will find it easier to move forward with conviction.

To become an efficacious investor, one must change one's mindset, beginning with training. Smaller steps with precise focal points—like saving goals and personal budgeting—should be implemented before larger investment plans are considered. Type Nine investors need to pace themselves so that confidence can grow in tandem with the complexity of tasks assumed.

FINDING PERSONAL INSPIRATION TO DEFINE INVESTING JOURNEYS

Type Nine investors must ask themselves what they want to accomplish on their financial journeys and be intentional in identifying their North Stars. A comfortable retirement may not be specific enough to jolt them into action. Goals for Type Nine investors should be more inspiring than that. Developing a mission statement—or statements—that can guide a life's purpose is ideal, but this can take many years to determine. I am still refining and rediscovering mine. Since Type Nines are typically not used to articulating the inner recesses of their beings, this process cannot be hurried.

HOMEOWNERSHIP AS A SOURCE OF PRIDE

An urgent and often evocative call to action for every Type Nine investor is to aim for homeownership while figuring out longer-term investment objectives and mission statements. Homeownership is a clear objective that one can visualize and a common enough goal that allows any Type Nine investor to go with the flow without feeling like an outlier. Targeting homeownership as a first investment milestone is an effective forcing function to compel personal action.

While some may think that renting accords greater flexibility, the overarching objective here is early empowerment. Owning one's home yields personal pride and self-possession, both essential ingredients of true inner peace. For Type Nine investors, the merits of owning a home extend beyond the financial; it is a stepping stone toward self-efficacy. In addition, accepting a long-term commitment to mortgage payments is symbolic of individual independence and financial discipline, qualities that will go a long way for Type Nine investors.

LOWER-RISK EXCHANGE-TRADED FUNDS

Saving for a down payment on a home should be the top priority for Type Nine investors. Investment risks must be approached cautiously because if markets turn and set a Type Nine investor back, it may affect confidence. Even the most popular stock index—the S&P 500—can fall by more than 10 percent in any given year during a bear market and stay depressed far longer than expected. Just look at 2001 to 2002, 2008, and 2022. Type Nine investors should move toward homeownership first without injecting unnecessary drama or uncertainties.

After the down payment and mortgage payments are accounted for, Type Nine investors may establish regular investment plans to build up their financial portfolios over multiple market cycles. These investments may be specific to certain industries, track broad-based equity indices, or lie in fixed income. Type Nine investors can flex discretionary muscles here to build diversified portfolios that reflect their instincts. Seeking professional opinions should be part of the process, but Type Nine investors must still make the ultimate decisions.

EXERCISE DISCRETION EARLY TO DEVELOP SELF-TRUST

Passivity is a double-edged sword for Type Nine investors. On the one hand, they do not panic and succumb to knee-jerk reactions. They are less likely to get swept up by FOMO in a bull market or cave to liquidation in a bear market. On the other hand, being too chill may devolve into burying one's head in the sand. A lack of decisive action can blunt instincts over time, robbing Type Nine investors of opportunities to build confidence and experience in managing portfolios over market cycles.

To strike the right balance, Type Nine investors can start exercising autonomy early regarding budgets, savings, repayment of student debt (if any), and investment options for their 401k plans. Once they start making money, Type Nine investors should tap into their Type One perfectionist wing to build structured financial hygiene. The more fiscal decisions they make, the better they will become at making them. Over time, Type Nine investors can progress to making more discretionary investments for their portfolios.

LIMITING PORTFOLIO EXPOSURE TO HIGHER-RISK ASSETS

With a natural tendency to look on the bright side to filter bad news, Type Nine investors may need to establish certain guardrails to avoid risky investments. While remaining calm in the face of volatility—and possessing steady hands to hold multigenerational winners like Starbucks and McDonald's—is essential, many individual stock investments go south or nowhere, like Yelp, GoPro, and Peloton. Maintaining a positive outlook to protect inner peace would have extracted a painful price in each of those instances.

Exercising discretion helps Type Nine investors remain connected with their instincts. When ready to expand beyond a lower-risk playbook (homeownership, fixed income, diversified equity, real estate, and gold), they may wish to allocate a limited portion of their portfolio (say 10 to 20 percent in portfolio capital outlays) toward discretionary investments.

APPOINT EXTERNAL ADVISERS

Working with external parties to perform reality checks on financial health requires a few qualifiers. First, Type Nine investors must be able to articulate their true objectives so that others may appreciate the nuances. The worst-case scenario is to have a Type Nine investor convey an inaccurate picture or a third party advocating a direction based on a misunderstanding. Second, Type Nine investors must feel comfortable expressing themselves to the appointed advisers. There needs to be an active dialogue. Type Nine investors must resist temptations to go with the flow, even if said advisers want to triangulate discussions quickly. Third, consider talking to disinterested third parties versus friends or relatives. Familiarity impedes Type Nine investors from sharing their inner thoughts and feelings for fear of contaminating relationships. Business and pleasure may not be a good mix for a Type Nine personality.

KEEP PURSUING FINANCIAL KNOW-HOW FOR SELF-IMPROVEMENT

Knowledge is power; it cannot be taken away by market forces. An essential companion on a Type Nine investor's investing journey is a learning routine that is conscious and intentional. And it is never too late. Type Nines possess strong instincts that can be reawakened through stimulating activities. Reading books on investing, listening to podcasts on financial literacy, initiating discussions with people, and signing up for relevant courses are some ways to acquire know-how. Leaning into their Type One wing to implement a discipline of lifelong learning builds self-confidence. Once they gain the basic knowledge and requisite experience through actions, Type Nines can be formidable investors. Uncanny instincts (regarding self and the financial world) can guide them toward seeding investments that blend well with their skills, interests, and personality profiles. The best of Type Nines invest with ease and natural endurance through the ups and downs of market cycles.

DEVELOPMENT PLAN FOR NINES: INTEGRATING TOWARD TYPE THREE (PERFORMER) AND TYPE SIX (SKEPTIC)

> **"And then I called Steve Jobs. It was an odd call to make, but it felt important to me to reach out to him, in case there might still someday be a chance of salvaging the relationship with Pixar."**
>
> *The Ride of a Lifetime* **by Robert Iger (2019)**

Robert Iger became the chief executive officer of the Walt Disney Company in 2005. One of his first calls as CEO was to Steve Jobs, then Pixar's controlling shareholder. His predecessor, Michael Eisner, and Jobs had been in an escalating feud, which ended the lucrative partnership between Walt Disney and Pixar.

In the early 2000s, Disney Animation was faltering after a series of box office flops and running out of creative juice. In contrast, Pixar was delighting audiences with computer animation hits like *Toy Story* (1995) and *The Incredibles* (2004). Even in public, Eisner and Jobs disliked each other and could not agree on coproduction and distribution terms beyond the original five-picture deal. In 2004, the partnership ended at an impasse.

Disney as a brand was at stake, given the importance of animation and how the company had trouble maintaining cultural relevance without having produced another *The Lion King* (1994), *Aladdin* (1992), or *The Little Mermaid* (1989) for years. The House of Mouse needed Pixar in order to make an existential leap into the future, but personality clashes prevented any deal from happening.

Instead of perpetuating the acrimony, Iger contacted Jobs to make peace. He set his ego aside to acknowledge how strategic Pixar was to Disney's future. Iger worked on the Apple founder with humility and a shrewd appreciation for what Jobs desired (respect from Disney and acknowledgment of Pixar's ingenuity). His initiative led to a reconciliation between the two companies and, eventually, the acquisition of Pixar by Disney in 2006. That groundbreaking deal secured Disney's future in animation more so than any conventional partnership could have delivered.

Without Iger inhabiting the role of a consummate Type Nine peacemaker, Disney might not have survived in the emerging world of three-dimensional computer graphics. That said, Iger did not just cave to what Jobs demanded; Pixar's original coproduction and distribution terms were as provocative as they would be damaging to Disney's bottom line. Iger's Type Nine instincts defended Disney's interests and guided him to strike a deal that exceeded all expectations, including his own.

Having led the Walt Disney Company for fifteen years, not including the additional years after he resumed his post in late 2022, Iger is known for some of the savviest acquisitions (including Pixar, Marvel, and Lucasfilm) in corporate history. In his autobiography, *The Ride of a Lifetime*, he demonstrates an uncanny ability to understand and merge different points of view. His empathy and focus on establishing win-win dynamics (versus ego-driven one-upmanship) was how he reengaged with Jobs, won his trust, and negotiated a combination between Disney and Pixar that no one thought possible.

Iger is a quintessential Type Nine peacemaker who has reached the pinnacle of success through astuteness, stamina, diplomacy, and exuberant charm—and without getting caught in a public feud with *Black Widow*.[1]

It is easy to pigeonhole Type Nine peacemakers as gentle, nurturing figures. True, there are similarities in terms of harmony and compassionate leadership—but that image can suggest a lack of personal power, especially compared to their instinctual cousins, the fiery Type Eight challengers and disciplined Type One perfectionists. This could not be further from the truth. The best Type Nines exude power. Just witness Iger, one of the most powerful figures in the entertainment industry.

---

1 Former chief executive officer Robert Chapek was entangled in a disagreement with actress Scarlett Johansson when her theatrical film, *Black Widow*, was released simultaneously on Disney+ in July 2021. She sued for breach of contract, and it escalated into a highly publicized lawsuit.

If world peace is indeed the ultimate human objective, Type Nines will be uniquely positioned to take over the world. Being an excellent peacemaker does not mean rolling over and going along with everyone. In fact, that is the worst strategy. We all have our thoughts, feelings, and instincts. Having the wisdom and fortitude to express them without letting our egos pervert or confuse our intentions is crucial to self-actualization. The best Type Nine peacemakers possess full vitality and a keen awareness of their personal priorities. Their superpowers stem from an unlabored ability to see multiple vantage points and intuit unspoken bargaining chips, limitations, leverage, and potential areas of compromise. As a result, they can move everyone forward in true unity and still advance their agenda.

To evolve to the levels of integration reached by the likes of Iger and Barack Obama (another model Type Nine) is not an easy task. Less healthy Type Nines, as children, often received the message to suppress their human spirit so as not to cause a disturbance. As a result, they grow up feeling less defined and incomplete.

To reclaim their essence, the Enneagram suggests two pivots. Assuming the taskmaster traits of Type Three performers will help reignite their thirst for life. The more Type Nines practice the habit of checking off items on their agenda, the more confident they will feel, pushing them to set even loftier goals. Establishing schedules ahead of time removes the need to make spontaneous decisions (which can be stressful for Type Nines) and minimizes the odds of procrastination. Soon, they will no longer be satisfied with laid-back indifference; healthier Type Nines will begin to find their inner strength to stay engaged and accomplish milestones with gumption.

The other pivot is that of a cerebral Type Six skeptic. Critical thinking purges mental passivity, allowing a Type Nine to elucidate multiple scenarios rather than subscribing to only platitudes, which Type Nines tend to employ in spades when facing difficult situations. This pivot applies to the perception of people as well. Humans come in shades of gray and are complex creatures with nuanced motivations. A degree of healthy skepticism mixed with curiosity provides a better counterbalance for these peacemakers. While optimism is an essential ingredient of life, Type Nines tend to abuse it like a drug to numb out instincts.

As Type Nines take control, especially of their personal investing journeys, they will be reawakened. They are just as capable of poise and power as everyone else. Equipped with innate instincts to navigate their inner and outer worlds, liberated Type Nines can find their niches to pursue individual purposes. When they are fully engaged with life, inner peace becomes a natural outcome, no longer an elusive goal.

Chapter 12

My Ongoing Enneagram and Financial Journey

"Snap out of it!"

Moonstruck (1987)

Have you convinced yourself not to do something, only to realize in retrospect that you should have done that very thing? As a Type Five (investigator), I identify with that pattern, given how my fear-driven unconscious can and did hold me back in the past. Taking steps out of our comfort zones requires real courage, and if left to our own devices, the nervous system can play tricks on us. It keeps us safe by recalling thoughts, feelings, and instincts to explain why we should maintain homeostasis. We are not inclined to initiate massive shocks to our paradigms, especially if there are no pressing push or pull factors to compel changes. Human beings are nothing if not consistent. Unless, of course, you identify as Madonna or Lady Gaga; then reinvention is scheduled for each album release cycle.

However, when significant pivots do happen—voluntarily or involuntarily—and we adopt traits outside our comfort zones, we often emerge more courageous, wiser, and more in touch with our feelings. Reflecting on my investing history, I have found my most significant Enneagram shifts and investing lessons were the product of unanticipated life events, for which I am grateful.

HOW MY UPBRINGING LED TO MY TYPOLOGY

My mother left soon after I was born. I will never know all the details of what happened since she passed before I had a chance to meet her. My father did not live with me until I was a young teenager. I grew up with few privileges in a two-bedroom government rental apartment with six adults (grandmother plus aunts and uncles) cramped together within it. Expressions of feelings were neither encouraged nor mirrored. I was extremely shy as a result. Perhaps the lack of living space also deterred movement, hence the action-center part of me was not nurtured. My mind became the only space to run free and be myself. Almost by process of elimination, a Type Five archetype soon emerged.

Specifically, a scarcity mindset from a fear of losing what little I had became prominent in my personality. Hoarding—my father, money, time, and other seemingly nonreplenishable resources—was a habit I adopted early on. I was self-sufficient for survival's sake, not for the sake of personal development or higher consciousness. That mentality permeated all aspects of my being until I became more self-aware after discovering the Enneagram while well into my third decade of life.

AT MY MOST INSULAR AS A TYPE FIVE

Ironically, my trademark Type Five scarcity mindset became most evident when I started working at an investment bank at twenty-four.[2] Before that, I worked hard in school and grew courage like a Type Eight (challenger) to network and take up space at every recruitment event. Like a Type Seven (enthusiast), I envisaged a brighter future for myself and chased after my dream with all the energy I could muster.

Once I got my foot in the door, however, I stopped taking risks. I was determined to conserve everything I had attained up to that

---

2   Like all male Singapore citizens and permanent residents, I had to serve two and a half years (recently reduced to two) in the military at age eighteen.

point. Instead of feeling secure (given how much more I had as a working adult than I did as a student or a child) and developing an abundant mindset, I became afraid to lose my new lease of life. I went on to define my entire identity by job performance.

Averaging a hundred hours a week as a corporate finance analyst was how I lived for years. I had no personal life because I did not believe I could achieve more. By focusing only on my job, I thought I could become immune to retrenchment, which was still possible in a post-dot-com bust. I held back from socializing, spending time with family, or meeting anyone during those years. It was a small life, though I did enjoy the accelerated learning and intellectual challenges at work, like a stereotypical Type Five.

Emotionally, though, I manifested fear, fueling the coffers of *Monsters, Incorporated*. No "scarer" needed; the fear was already inside me.

FRUGALITY OR JUST BEING A SCROOGE?

From youth, frugality was instilled in me. Being economical is a personal (and often unconscious) virtue that I continue to be proud of, but it can be taken too far. Being too driven by preservation has created hurdles, compromising learning and living gracefully.

In some twisted way, even with a healthy salary and healthier bonuses, fishing for bargains provided a more satisfying dopamine hit than partaking in spending patterns typical of a young, single banker living in Singapore. I would challenge myself to save more each month, which was easy since I still lived at my family home. I eschewed travel, fancy cars, and branded clothing. I did not even treat myself to an iPod when everyone around me had one. I prided myself on sticking with a Sony Discman.

Talk about masochism. I must have loved it. I minimized my needs and hoarded almost every penny, and it made me feel good. Discipline gave me a sense of control, and seeing those figures in my bank account made me feel secure. However, I did (and still do) provide meaningful financial support to my family and fund their vacations since they had limited resources to enjoy traveling. Other than that, I was wound up so tight I am surprised I did not implode. Even with my dream job, I was at my unhealthiest as a Type Five.

MY INITIAL INVESTMENTS: TREASURIES AND FIXED DEPOSITS

Until the first seismic change at age twenty-seven, I did not invest my money. I chose to keep everything in cash and government treasuries. When colleagues encouraged me to invest in properties, I rationalized—with a hint of self-righteousness—that I did not believe in taking on debt. I must have been insufferable.

Even though I worked in corporate finance and we were advising companies to raise and allocate capital toward growth through mergers and acquisitions and other expansion initiatives, my ethos reflected none of that. I was holding my money at almost zero returns. I did not practice what we were preaching as an advisory firm. I did not possess a growth mindset. Because I was so afraid to lose what I had worked so hard for, I did not retain the courageous (Type Eight challenger) and visionary (Type Seven enthusiast) traits I demonstrated when I was gunning for my dream job. I went back to my original Type Five prototype and just worked hard. I had no idea of the genuine treasures waiting to be explored in the outside world.

MY FIRST LARGE INVESTMENT: A PERSONAL LAIR

Having been raised in a country where male homosexuality was illegal until 2022, I grew up in shame and fear over my sexuality. Still, I was never more self-conscious than I was early in my career. I had more balls as a young teen, chasing boys in my secondary school and embracing Madonna as my fairy godmother. I did not experience any pressure to date girls (or pretend to), partly because my family did not expect me to settle down. My father was already a cautionary tale for marrying too young. Besides, I did not grow up in the presence of heterosexual parents to model myself after.

Things changed when I joined the workforce. Even though I was working in an international bank, surrounded by many open-minded expatriates, that fear over what would happen if I came out of the closet lingered. There were undoubtedly LGBTQIA+ people being ostracized in professional and social circles in Singapore, and homophobic remarks were uttered at my workplace multiple times. The fearful way I responded, however, was disproportionate to the actual risk to my career or acceptance by my colleagues. By my own doing, I alienated myself further. Every time there was a conversation about relationships, I got awkward. I did not want to disclose my sexuality. Withholding personal information was another hallmark Type Five personality trait I embodied back then.

I was doing well professionally, and my work was appreciated and rewarded. I grew richer financially, but my connections—and inner life—had never been so poor. Personally, I rejected myself and the concept of abundance. I had abandoned the real me. I could have garnered more fulfillment and balance in life had I pushed myself to connect with people, both at work and outside of it.

At twenty-seven, however, a major change happened. I went from being someone only willing to invest his money in fixed deposits and treasuries to emptying my bank account to buy a condominium without hesitation. No, I did not take cocaine or make a quantum leap in consciousness through divine epiphany. The motivation was far more straightforward and basic.

Sex.

Or first love, to be less crude.

Up until then, I was living with my family and working nonstop. My motivation to move out was zero. In Singapore, the prevailing culture among locals is to continue living with families until one gets married. That would never happen since I was gay. Nobody in my family was kicking me out, either.

As a Type Five, I did not feel the need to compare myself with my investment banking peers who were already living in their own apartments, buying properties, and investing in stocks. My focus was more insular: accumulating more expertise in my job. In hindsight, I was dominated by fear of taking action outside the comfort zone of my job. I rationalized everything I was not doing: investing, exercising, meditating, dating, reading anything unrelated to corporate finance, personal grooming, traveling, socializing, or networking. I chose to work even over holidays like Chinese New Year and Christmas. At most, I would take a few days off, check into a local luxury hotel, and read books like *Valuation: Measuring and Managing the Value of Companies* by McKinsey & Company.

Meanwhile, many of my colleagues were both working and playing hard, taking full advantage of Singapore's proximity to nearby resort islands and zero-capital-gains tax policies. There were always compelling reasons (or excuses, in retrospect) not to do something because I needed to focus on getting more familiar with *The Singapore Code on Take-overs and Mergers* or reading back issues of *International Financing Review Asia*. Because I was also afraid of being outed at work, I held back from joining dating apps. One of my biggest fears then was a colleague sharing a screenshot of me on Grindr in mockery or spotting me at a gay bar. It sounds silly now, but that was an expression of a fear-driven, unhealthy Type Five.

Thanks to my primal instincts and repressed need to be loved, those lifestyle habits were soon to be broken. My hormones took over, and I started sneaking into gay bars like an adventurous Type Seven. A few weeks after coming out of my self-imposed shell, I met someone in the summer of 2006. His name was Joseph, and he was the catalyst I needed to make major transformations in my life.

All that pent-up desire for love, support, and comfort bubbled to the surface, and within weeks, I wanted my own space to take Joseph home to. It did not matter that he was a complete psychopath. He was cute, and it was a done deal. In that department, I pivoted to the lowest form of a Type Seven enthusiast, jumping straight to the altar in my mind. The idea of living with him in my apartment took hold quicker than the time needed to build a discounted cash flow model, which I had mastered by then. I did not tap into my Type Six wing of skepticism to consider if the relationship was even right. My enthusiastic pushback against extreme repression had the effect of overriding any hesitation, and I was full of urgency. I could not wait to leave my family home, and my mind was filled with optimistic visions of how my new life would be with my new boyfriend.

My Type Eight (challenger) pivot kicked into high gear by instinct, marshaling my cousin Karine (whom I grew up with and trusted) to help me find suitable properties. The process came together in record time since I acted like a decisive Type Eight investor. There was no fear of buying the wrong property or whether my job was stable enough to support the mortgage. I took charge, was assured of my ability to take on the added financial responsibility, and was ready to plunge into a new life. If I had been my usual Type Five self, I would have kept looking for options and drawn up a spreadsheet of comparable properties. Instead, I saw the first condominium, which Karine had learned about from a friend, and that was it. I did not scout alternatives because that property had a great location, the price was right, and my gut said yes. Game on.

I made the down payment in the late summer of 2006 and started remodeling. Meanwhile, I continued seeing Joseph, but the relationship grew rocky after a short honeymoon phase. By the time the place was ready, I was no longer seeing him. Around Christmas 2006, I moved into my new abode alone. I remember spending my first night there wondering what I had done to myself. Everything felt strange and surreal. My bubble burst; my first love story was a tragic dark comedy.

But Joseph appeared in my life for a reason: He was the forcing function I needed. I had beginner's luck with the property because real estate prices in Singapore were just at the cusp of hyperbolic appreciation. This purchase marked the first significant step on my financial journey, and the condominium unit would become a meaningful addition to my portfolio. Living alone was character building as well, giving me space to become more confident as a person and investor.

FEAR OF TECHNOLOGY AND THE UNKNOWN OUTSIDE OF MY HOME COUNTRY

When I was growing up, gaining fluency in English was a real struggle compared to subjects like mathematics and science. I did not speak much English at home or in school. For years, I felt embarrassed by my lack of linguistic skills and avoided speaking (or writing) English as much as possible. It was not until my teens that I leaned into confronting the one academic weakness pulling down my grade point average.

When it comes to investing, I have gone through a similar trajectory. It may sound ironic because, as a Type Five investor, I should be on an insatiable path to acquiring knowledge like an investigative sponge. Yet fear lurks in my psyche, and anything outside of my comfort zone can be considered unsafe, including learning intimidating subject matters.

Unsurprisingly, when I started building an equity portfolio in my thirties, I homed in on Singapore-based companies rather than multinationals like Apple or even Exxon Mobil, where I interned during my university days. My own backyard felt most familiar, so I didn't bother discussing investment opportunities with coworkers (many of whom had more experience with personal investing) or getting curious about global companies that were changing the world. I thought I was conserving what I believed to be limited resources—time and money—by focusing only on companies that were operating on my home turf. Looking back, I robbed myself of the opportunity to explore more exciting and cutting-edge enterprises outside of Singapore.

Technology was the area I avoided the most during my earlier days as a Type Five investor. I feared it, and for quite a few years, I even avoided using internet banking. I tend to stick to what I already know, which corroborates nicely with a key Type Five feature (more like a bug, really) of being insular. I would rather divorce myself from technology and not deal with it than put on my curiosity hat to find out how it could augment my equity portfolio. I could have learned more about e-commerce, Silicon Valley, financial technology, streaming, and software as a service in the early 2000s, but instead, I stayed as far away from these concepts as possible.

PURE VALUE INVESTING AS A TYPE FIVE

I still remember a chance meeting with a private banker from Hong Kong in 2014. I was traveling through Italy on a break after eleven years of working at Credit Suisse. She and I were talking about financial independence, and I shared my approach as a value investor with her. By then, I had amassed a portfolio of dividend-paying Singapore-based companies as a bargain hunter, with two investment properties generating rental income. She brought up Tesla and Elon Musk, two names foreign to me. Intrigued, I returned to my hotel room and looked at Tesla's financial filings like a diligent Type Five investor. I was immediately horrified by the income statement and cash flow profile—all losses! After a cursory glance, I dismissed that idea altogether and reverted to the mental safety of value investing. It was not until early 2019 that I would look at Tesla again.

Value investing has a lot in common with a Type Five mindset. This is not a dismissal of the approach but rather an observation of how it resonates best with this archetype. Using multiples—such as price-to-earnings, price-to-revenue, and price-to-book ratios—derived from reported or guided financial figures provides one with mental comforts when making investment decisions because the inputs are known quantities. Concomitant with value investing is eliminating companies trading at sky-high valuations. A high tolerance of uncertainty is required when investing in fast growers since one needs to make bold assumptions about future cash flow from potential businesses that may or may not work out. Value investing does not extrapolate that far and only focuses on companies trading at reasonable levels. This is Type Five thinking without a concurrent Type Seven pivot: safe and conservative, sans future-oriented outlook.

Limiting downside risks is a crucial bedrock of value investing, and this also rhymes with the scarcity mindset that defines Type Five personalities. We want to conserve our capital and not risk losing our financial resources, lest our independence or ability to survive isolation be threatened. We do not want to be seen as foolishly overpaying for anything. Addressing the downside risk through value investing mitigates the fears that Type Five investors tend to have.

As a resource hoarder, I have always been drawn to the so-called underpriced companies, much like a prudent person fishing for bargains at a discount store. There are certainly opportunities in the market when companies can trade at massive, irrational discounts, but most of the time, they do not. There are good reasons why many companies trade at discounts; they are known as value traps due to declining prospects. Highfliers are rarely found in bargain bins.

Going back to Tesla, it would never have been screened as a value stock for me in 2014. Even after it was included in the S&P 500 index in December 2020, valuation multiples were well above traditional automotive makers. Many successful companies trade at seemingly expensive levels, except perhaps during economic downturns. Nonetheless, during turbulent times, the fear of losing everything is even more amplified in those who are already afraid; more likely than not, capital is further held back for conservation versus actual bottom fishing.

PIVOTING TO A GROWTH MINDSET WITH GROWTH STOCKS

"Book value can go to zero," said my soon-to-be husband, Blake, with an eye roll. He is an American and a sarcastic one.

There was a time when I was obsessed with the price-to-net tangible asset ratio and would screen for stocks on Bloomberg terminals accordingly. I believed in Benjamin Graham's *The Intelligent Investor* and trusted the process prescribed by the book, partly because it was logical and partly because it felt safe to limit the downside by relying on known elements from financial statements.

Blake was a different breed of investor. He did not do any screening based on multiples but would invest in companies he felt were changing the world or had the potential to become big. Although we were both in banking and well acquainted with all sorts of valuation techniques, our approaches could not be more different when putting our money to work. Blake is a Type Three investor who relies on his emotions to make financial decisions more than he can admit. He was born and raised in America, and investing in American companies is second nature to him. So, throughout his banking career (first in New York, then Singapore), he invested in the likes of Apple, Facebook, VMware, and Google with his bonuses.

American companies did not appeal to me because none of those big names traded at attractive enough valuations, so I convinced myself not to bother. Besides, I was intimidated by the unknown nature of foreign companies. Many prominent ones then were also technology heavy, and I made up even more excuses to stay within my home turf. The mind can rationalize whatever it needs to insulate oneself within a perceived safety zone. In doing so, I limited my learning opportunities a great deal.

There is no prize for guessing who did better with stocks during those years.

When he learned about my approach to investing in Singapore companies, he dismissed it sarcastically, and I was upset. My initial response was to shut him down and stick my head in the sand—or, more precisely, into the pages of *The Intelligent Investor*. How dare he say book value could go to zero, I thought. Beyond my indignation, I did not further contemplate book value or what he meant. It was a while before I became more influenced by his perspectives. I was lucky I did not marry a fellow Type Five investor; otherwise, I would not have reevaluated my investment philosophy.

The first growth story I bought into was Match Group in 2018. By then, Tinder was already raging among younger folks. I was unaware of the application until 2015 when I started working at UBS and connected with younger bankers. By 2018, Match Group had just turned profitable, but it was still considered expensive under traditional value investing standards; book value was a mere fraction of market capitalization. Investing in Match Group was a drastic departure for me but the exact first step I needed to snap out of my ultraconservative and fear-driven value-investing style. After Match Group, I started to deploy more capital toward fast-growing consumer and technology names in America and Europe. It was the beginning of a more abundant style of thinking.

Looking back, my most significant changes as an investor have been the results of penetrating—if not slightly rattling—interactions with people from different backgrounds. It is an effective forcing function to detach from the internalized thinking models that I am prone to. In other words, my investing journey has involved pivoting toward a Type Eight (challenger): garnering self-assurance to change, pushing against resistance (including self), establishing connections, and opening to abundance (versus Type Five scarcity). It also took leaning into a Type Seven (enthusiast) persona: imagining what the future looks like beyond the obvious, extrapolating from the growing pains that manifest in financial statements, and desiring more than just to take advantage of market dislocations in the bargain bins.

Value investing comes easier to my Type Five personality, which desires safety with known quantities. On the other hand, growth investing requires projecting into the future, garnering external viewpoints, and daring to postulate. It requires a leap of faith, for which Type Seven enthusiasts and Type Eight challengers have a most excellent flair.

BIGGEST INVESTING MISTAKES MADE AND LESSONS LEARNED

Luck plays a significant role in investing. In fact, luck—also known as divine intervention, being in the right place at the right time, fate, and so on—plays a role in everything. No investor can forecast the outcome of any investee company, even if it is led by certifiable geniuses. In the book *Shoe Dog*, Nike founder Phil Knight recounts multiple near-death experiences that almost killed the company during its earlier days as Blue Ribbon Sports. Nike would not be the juggernaut it is today were it not for plenty of serendipity. Being open-minded to opportunities that luck brings is essential. Without a receptive mind, a connected heart, and the willingness to act, luck would pass us by, even if it was right in front of us.

As a Type Five investor, I tend to overestimate my cerebral prowess, which can be a slippery slope. Initial successes, especially if fueled by plenty of luck, can embolden one to take riskier bets. Those can become expensive pitfalls. We are all subject to self-serving biases. I have had successes that could have gone the other way, but they did not, and I became convinced that I was the MVP of individual investing until I had my ego taken down a notch or two. No buy or short thesis is bulletproof. Something can always go wrong; black swans (for example, the dot-com bust, the 2008 global financial crisis, COVID-19, unexpected legal rulings against a company, and antitrust changes) are real. This does not suggest that we should constantly look for worst-case scenarios. Yet we must be informed by possibilities, and diversification is essential.

Let's return to John Maynard Keynes's famous saying, "Markets can stay irrational longer than investors can remain solvent," which I take to heart. I have never taken on leverage against my equity portfolio, because margin calls can happen at the worst possible times. I remember computing multimillion-dollar cash calls while working in the loans division at Credit Suisse during the crash of 2007 to 2008. Many of the bank's clients took massive leverage secured against baskets of assets deemed safe, only to see their market values plummet during that period.

Below are key lessons I have learned as a Type Five investor.

REITS: MARKET VALUES CAN FALL AS HARD AS STOCKS

After owning two condos and being hit by a soft rental market, I decided that having most of my passive cash flow tied to just two tenancies was not a viable strategy. At one point, the larger unit was vacant for six months, and while I had a sufficient cash buffer (being Type Five conservative with cash and mortgages helped), the lesson was clear.

Residential properties in Singapore had benefited from a boom in the early 2000s, and I caught a wave of appreciation in 2006 and again in 2011. Rental yields, however, were compressed, and overseas investors were bidding up home prices even more. Because my units were larger, finding tenants was not as easy. So, in 2017, I decided to recycle my capital into REITs. I reasoned that they comprised the same underlying asset class but with a much more diversified tenant base. Besides, distributions were tax-free—versus taxable rental income—in Singapore. While it improved my cash flow and saved me a ton of headaches from dealing with individual tenancy issues, I did not fully appreciate the nuances of owning multiple REITs. Some healthy skepticism from my Type Six wing would have been helpful in that situation, but I was too impatient to contemplate multiple scenarios.

Even though I had purchased what I believed to be the largest and most reputable of REITs, prices were nevertheless volatile. When they wavered, my gut went for a wilder ride than I was ready for. Moreover, my universe of risk factors expanded substantially because of the multitude of property classes underlying my REIT portfolio—commercial, retail, hospitality, and logistics—and geographical exposures. For example, when a series of demonstrations hit Hong Kong between 2019 and 2020 in response to the introduction of the fugitive offenders amendment bill, all hell broke loose in the city. Retail properties were torched, looted, and vandalized. One of those—Festival Walk—was an anchor asset owned by a REIT in my portfolio. That was not a happy outcome.

When COVID-19 hit in 2020, it was painful to watch my entire real estate portfolio melt away. It did not matter if a REIT was backed by the largest institutional pension funds or if the most creditworthy tenants occupied the underlying assets. COVID-19 hit commercial, retail, and hospitality assets especially hard, and those were some of the most stressful months of my life as an investor. I did take advantage of bargain hunting during that period, but it was still nerve-racking. Eventually, many of them recovered, and I rebalanced my portfolio. COVID-19 demonstrated that stocks—no matter the underlying business or asset compositions—are volatile, and one must have the stomach for it. When it comes to real estate, a mix of direct ownership and REITs would have been a better approach.

OVERCONFIDENCE FROM TESLA: SUCCESS BIAS

Tesla has been my most satisfying investment to date, but it also cascaded into overconfidence on my part.

In early 2019, when I was visiting my husband in Atlanta, Georgia, Tesla was all over the news for the wrong reasons. Attention was not on the revolutionary electric vehicles rolling out of the Tesla Fremont

Factory but on troubles brewing inside and outside the company. Tesla was in production hell trying to ramp up Model 3, designed for the much larger mass market versus prior models (Roadster, Model X, and Model S) priced at the higher end for niche customers. Though settled, fraud charges by the Securities and Exchange Commission against Elon Musk remained topical and reflected poorly on him. Elsewhere, celebrity fund managers Jim Chanos and David Einhorn were decrying Tesla stock across media channels to support their short positions. Negativity against Tesla was in vogue. Despite all that, we arranged to test-drive the Model 3 and loved it. Subsequently, we invested in Tesla stock and held on for a rough ride as market sentiment worsened and its stock price fell by half.

Fast-forward a couple of years, and Tesla became one of the most valuable companies in the world. I was emboldened and became convinced I could beat the markets. So I pivoted more toward growth stocks, especially in the consumer and technology sectors. I went from investing in properties and Singapore companies using price-to-book ratios to the far end of growth investing. I was diving into the technology ocean for software, e-commerce, fintech, advertising technology, social media, and cloud computing. I stretched my learning and enjoyed it, making many good investments along the way. Still, I pivoted too far and left some essential value-investing ethos behind. When 2022 came around, my portfolio (and ego) took a severe beating.

When Tesla had major issues ramping up Model 3, Elon Musk described the company as edging close to bankruptcy. If it had not succeeded in overcoming complex production issues, Tesla would be worth only a tiny fraction of what it is today. In other words, I was lucky with my Tesla investment, though I do give myself credit for doing my homework on the company. I also pat myself on the back for hanging on to my Tesla stock and thesis—which I updated, analyzed, and reanalyzed for every corporate development—with steadfast conviction, even as Tesla stock was under attack by naysayers, bearish analysts, self-anointed stock gurus, and vicious journalists.

Regardless, luck played a big part. I did not possess any automotive knowledge and certainly had zero clue as to what specific manufacturing complications or vexations Tesla faced at that time with the Model 3 ramp. I invested (and held on) because I liked the vehicle, valuation multiples based on sales were reasonable, and I was drawn to Musk as a personality. In other words, I had a blue-sky scenario in my head—like a Type Seven enthusiast investor—and proceeded more on faith than the cautious skepticism that my Type Six wing would have exerted.

That worked out, but when rinsed and repeated elsewhere, the same approach backfired in some cases.

PELOTON: MY ASS GOT WHOOPED

When Peloton became public in September 2019, I was not keen on the stock since spinning did not interest me. Even prepandemic, the buzz was undeniable. Peloton was the first mover in the connected fitness space, and its bikes appealed to many customers, who became devotees. The company was not shy about brand building.

After they opened a store in Marylebone, London, close to where I lived, I signed up for a live class at their London studio. It was free to participate, so why not? Off I went, and it was a great experience. I even returned for another session. Many riders there were fanatical users of their bikes at home.

Shortly after the pandemic hit and shares were all trading at historic lows, I started building a small position in Peloton. It appeared to check all the boxes of a future giant in the consumer space: founder-led management, evocative brand, growing fan base, and innovation. Sure, one could dismiss Peloton as a stationary bike with an iPad attached, but most successful brands in the consumer space, like Nike and Lululemon, do not make rocket ships either. Irresistible product image and deep customer connections are keys to success for lifestyle-led brands, and Peloton excelled on both fronts.

As Peloton continued selling more bikes, issues at the company started to surface. My mistake with Peloton was ignoring the major red flags for too long throughout 2021. That was my unhealthy insular Type Five personality at work. Their escalating costs, multiple debacles with their line of treadmills, and capital raise in late 2021 were canaries in a coal mine. I have a strict limit on the amount of capital deployed to any single name, so I did not add excessively to my diversified portfolio. That cap saved me from doing dollar-cost averaging when Peloton was heading south.

I eventually sold out in early 2022, a tad late, but I was relieved that I did. Peloton would continue to struggle, even after multiple equity and debt capital raises. It was surreal to witness an increased demand discombobulating its operations to the point where Peloton had to abandon its vertically integrated strategy. Starting in 2022, it would rely solely on original equipment manufacturers.

STAYING PRESENT WITH AN ABUNDANT MINDSET

> **"God, grant me the serenity to accept the things I cannot change, the courage to change the things I can, and the wisdom to know the difference."**
>
> *Serenity Prayer*

I have always been in awe of people with the faith and fortitude to live in the present, seemingly without the fear of failure. Especially college graduates—or dropouts—who resist the temptation of joining management consulting, investment banking, or Big Tech to carve out their niches. Whenever I recall the likes of Bill Gates or Mark Zuckerberg and visualize the chronology of what they have accomplished, something inside me surges and makes me teary-eyed. They displayed such immense courage and self-belief so early in adulthood, daring to pursue their dreams. These icons eschew scarcity to embody abundance in mindset.

I cannot change the past that molded the first iterations of my personality. I am Type Five, partly due to my childhood and upbringing. Earlier choices were made from an overall theme of lack and were the best I could have made without the benefit of the self-awareness I now possess. Over the years, I have become more observant of the fears inside me and how they relate to the past. This knowledge has helped me become more assertive, take risks, and connect with people. Whenever I choose not to do something, I contemplate whether I am mission-focused or merely fearful of the unknown. My increasing action bias and connection to my emotional faculties are qualities I practice daily as a counterbalance to living in my head. I continue to be intentional—growing in courage (Type Eight), sharpening my vision (Type Seven), and becoming more discerning (Type Six) while developing compassion for myself on this personal investing journey.

A vital virtue I have been focusing on cultivating is contentment. Greed comes with an overriding acquisitiveness, compromising our clarity and distorting our nervous system. Personal investing is a lifelong journey, and we should enjoy it versus being plagued by depressive or anxious thoughts. A reasonable degree of self-understanding is essential to knowing whether the investing road map chosen is the right one at each point.

In the last few years, I have learned through my investing journey that I have a large void in my heart. As a Type Five, I desire self-sufficiency because I suffer from childhood abandonment and post-traumatic stress disorder. I first tried to fill that void with academic grades, then corporate titles and money, but the more I discovered myself, the more I understood that only love could fill that void. Multibaggers in my portfolio are great for my sense of accomplishment but do not plug the larger emotional holes. Since seeking help in my late thirties, I have addressed some complex core issues.

The way I have learned to manage personal investing runs in parallel to my personal growth. I started out investing only in treasuries due to a real fear of taking risks, then pivoted to become more open-minded, seeking equilibrium among new learnings, higher returns, and measured prudence. Changes to my portfolio composition over the years reflect my personal evolution. With growing confidence and inspiration from alternative perspectives, I have adopted more Type Seven (enthusiast) and Type Eight (challenger) traits to become bolder in pursuing my vision, which extends beyond numbers. No longer just motivated by fear, I want to create a different future for myself, one that is not tied to the ghost of my past but rather driven by a future that lies in the present hands of my inner child.

EPILOGUE

In early 2023, as I was completing this manuscript, I could not have anticipated the changes that would soon reshape my life. At the time, I was beginning to confront long-held issues from my past and noticed subtle yet significant shifts in my personality. No longer content with the intellectual isolation and self-preservation that defined my Type Five origins, I felt an undeniable pull toward deeper connection and purpose. Perhaps driven by an unconscious yearning for answers, I enrolled in graduate school that summer to study clinical mental health counseling.

Through my blog and FinTwit engagements, I met another writer, Sam Fargo. After coauthoring an article on the Walt Disney Company and becoming friends, we discovered a shared passion for the intersection of technology and psychology. This collaboration eventually led to the founding of Psyntel, a software company harnessing artificial intelligence to empower mental health professionals. Our personal experiences with trauma inspired us to meaningfully address the mental health crisis in a postpandemic world. I also joined the board of PEACE, a nonprofit organization providing pro bono therapy to Asian American and Pacific Islander communities in Georgia, further solidifying my commitment to service and healing.

The most life-changing moment came on February 4, 2024, when my husband and I became first-time fathers to our son, Paxton. Parenthood redefined my world in ways I could never have imagined, bringing profound joy while challenging me to grow across the Enneagram spectrum. In preparation for fatherhood, I approached the unknown with a meticulous Type One focus, devouring baby books to equip myself with the rules of newborn care. When our surrogate was diagnosed with preeclampsia, I leaned on Type Six grounded reasoning by relying not only on the guidance of the care team but also on my friends in the medical field to seek additional viewpoints and address my anxiety.

When Paxton finally arrived, I embraced the intuitive strength of my Type Eight pivot with courage and conviction. Parenthood pushed me beyond my usual self-focus, allowing me to embody a nurturing Type Two generosity and prioritize the well-being of my son and husband as we adapted to a new way of life. In the emotional turbulence of our newly expanded household, I called on the harmonizing energy of my inner Type Nine to manage conflicts and the reflective depth of my Type Four wing to process my evolving inner world. My Type Five intellect proved invaluable for decoding Paxton's cues and solving daily challenges, while my achievement-driven Type Three energy fueled my diligent tracking of his developmental milestones. Most importantly, I inhabited the optimism of a Type Seven to maintain positivity through those demanding early months—an outlook I strive to sustain every day.

Fatherhood has filled an amorphous void within me, replacing it with contentment, gratitude, and indescribable joy. It has taught me that growth is not just about mastering tasks or achieving goals but also about expanding into new dimensions of connection and love.

PORTFOLIO EVOLUTION AND EATING MY DOG FOOD

As my husband and I prepared for parenthood, we also decided it was time to find a larger home, one more conducive to raising a child. We had been living in a townhome purchased in early 2021 with a mortgage costing less than 3 percent. By early 2024, borrowing rates had soared to nearly 8 percent, and taking on a substantial loan based on conventional 80 percent leverage felt excessive, even if our income could support it. To lighten the financial load, I offered to liquidate part of my stock portfolio to raise more equity for the purchase.

As someone with a Type Five personality, who tends to minimize rather than maximize lifestyle, I would not have initiated the home purchase. But I did it for our family, and in doing so, I found a compelling reason to reevaluate my entire portfolio. Deciding which positions to sell became an exercise in applying the Enneagram investing lessons I had written about—and taking my own advice.

Realizing that my portfolio had become overexposed to smaller capitalization stocks, the type that often appeals to my intellectual tendencies, I prioritized liquidating those positions first. While this decision was practical, it was not without regret. Some stocks I sold have since performed exceptionally well, significantly surpassing my disposal price. Detaching myself from value stocks (or traps) that appeared attractive based on multiple valuation metrics also proved challenging. For instance, I decided to sell Match Group, a company that had struggled for several quarters as Tinder failed to grow its user base. Match Group held sentimental value for me, being the first growth stock I purchased in 2018, but its evolving business dynamics no longer aligned with my investment thesis. Letting it go required confronting my intrinsic inertia and reluctance to part with familiar holdings—a difficult but necessary step in creating a more intentional portfolio.

Ultimately, this experience forced me to assess how my Type Five tendencies were serving or sabotaging my goals. Concentrating my portfolio on larger, more established companies was not just a practical response to life circumstances but also a deliberate effort to avoid the intellectual allure of speculative investments. After the restructuring, my assets were anchored by home equity, while my liquid investments were evenly spread across S&P 500 constituent stocks, REITs, cash, fixed income, and companies poised for index inclusion. I continue to build on this foundation with regular contributions, mindful of my blind spots and biases.

In another significant shift, my husband and I are hiring a

financial adviser. For someone who once prided himself on DIY investing, this decision felt like stepping outside my comfort zone. Yet it aligns perfectly with my advice to Type Five investors: Seek perspectives beyond your own. It is not about relinquishing control but rather about expanding understanding—gaining new insights to complement strengths and cover weaknesses.

Following my advice has been humbling and liberating. The road map I laid out for Type Five investors—diversification, periodic purging, and collaboration—has been my guiding star. Whether cutting losses, resisting value traps, or acknowledging that others might know something I do not, these principles have helped me navigate my natural tendencies to overanalyze and retreat into intellectual isolation.

This journey has also reminded me that personal investing, like life, is dynamic. It requires us to adapt, recalibrate, and occasionally admit we are wrong. As a Type Five, stepping away from the mental fortress I built for myself feels counterintuitive. Yet doing so has allowed me to create something better: a portfolio—and a life—rooted in balance, intention, and growth.

So, yes, I am eating my own dog food. And I must say, it tastes pretty good.

CLOSING THOUGHTS

Each change I have made in life has deepened my understanding of intentional investing, broadening my perspective beyond financial goals to embrace a richer and more meaningful way of living. In *Man's Search for Meaning*, Viktor Frankl reminds us that purpose is not found in possessions but in aligning our actions with values that transcend self-interest. Even in the darkest times, Frankl found strength in a sense of mission—a lesson that resonates with me. His insight has profoundly shaped my investment philosophy and broader life choices, encouraging me to align resources with values to create meaningful impact. True wealth lies in using what is available to build a future that reflects our potential, strengthens communities, and leaves a legacy. With this ethos in mind, I hope *Suit Yourself*, alongside my entrepreneurial and nonprofit endeavors, contributes meaningfully to broader causes, making a difference where it is needed most.

This journey has also led me to explore Austrian doctor Alfred Adler's concept of the three life tasks, which align with the Enneagram's emphasis on balance and growth, offering a complementary perspective on living a full life. Adler proposed that contentment requires cultivating three essential areas of one's life: building a community (social task), establishing intimacy (love/marriage task), and contributing to society (occupational task). He argued that imbalance in these areas often results in discomfort and a lack of satisfaction.

As a Type Five, my natural inclination has been toward solitude and intellectual pursuits—seeking security in knowledge and withdrawing from emotional engagement. However, I have come to understand that true happiness lies in building relationships and contributing tangibly to the world around me.

Adopting Adler's framework meant leaning into the more extroverted traits of my Type Seven and Eight pivots. By consciously stepping out of my comfort zone, I strengthened family ties, built meaningful friendships, and collaborated with others across multiple endeavors. Just as a well-diversified portfolio mitigates risk and ensures sustainability, a well-rounded life integrates all its dimensions—community, intimacy, and contribution—for lasting fulfillment and resilience.

To my readers, I hope this book inspires you to align your investing strategies with your core strengths while recognizing the importance of balance and growth. Whether you are a Type Three seeking achievement, a Type Nine striving for peace, or a Type Two driven by helping others, investing can reflect your highest ideals. But as Frankl and Adler remind us, financial success alone does not sate our deepest yearnings. Meaning arises when we transcend self-interest to seek something larger.

Investing is just one facet of a well-lived life. I have learned that true abundance comes not from accumulation but from actively using what we possess to create, connect, and contribute. Creation offers a sense of accomplishment that no financial metric can provide, whether it be expressed through building a business, nurturing a family, or championing a cause. As humans, we are also hardwired to connect. Relationships—romantic, familial, professional, and communal—are the foundation of a fulfilling existence. By balancing ambition with a commitment to something greater, we invest not just in wealth but in life itself.

With new, expansive chapters of life unfolding, I aim to live a life where wealth is a means, not an end. For a Type Five like me, the tendency to hoard knowledge, energy, or money can feel like a safety net but ultimately limits growth. My hope is that you too discover an investment approach that reflects your unique personality while serving a higher purpose.

How can your investments reflect the best of who you are? Let us invest not only in assets but also in meaning, relationships, and a future that embodies our highest values.

ACKNOWLEDGMENTS

Writing this book has been a journey of discovery, perseverance, and connection. What began on a whim shortly after moving to the US in 2021 evolved into an experience that helped me establish roots in unfamiliar territory. At times, the process helped me combat loneliness in a new environment; at others, it was fueled by a conviction to share a concept I believed could genuinely resonate with the world.

First and foremost, my deepest gratitude goes to my husband, Blake, who has been my unwavering partner in this endeavor: From reviewing query letters and proposals to offering thoughtful insights into the earliest drafts of my manuscript, your support has been indispensable. Our marriage has been a catalyst for growth and change, and I am endlessly grateful for the love and strength we share.

To my literary agent, Leticia Gomez, whom I met serendipitously at the Atlanta Writers Conference: Thank you for believing in me and this book. Your confidence opened doors I never imagined possible, making this journey a reality.

I am profoundly grateful to my dear friend Shakuntala Chandramohan for the encouragement, positivity, and invaluable feedback on the manuscript. Your perspective and thoughtful suggestions enriched the work in countless ways.

To my friends who graciously supported this project in various ways, including taking my personality quiz, sharing their personal investing approaches, providing feedback, helping me make social media connections, and cheering me on: Adinda Bakrie, Amy Lee,

Dave Ahern, David Boggs, David Sexton, Duncan Brown, Elliott Wu, Eunji Ju, Felicia Teng, Joey Halloway, Karina Kho, Kevin Damaso, Nathan Worden, Patrick Kielly, Sean Alexander Huebner, Selina Barry, Sung Lee, Tim Tjendra, Tricia Kho, Winnie Kho, and Yoomin Hong. Your openness and generosity contributed depth and authenticity to this book.

I extend heartfelt thanks to the team at Integrative Enneagram Solutions, Dr. R. Karl Hebenstreit and Reverend Michelle Thomas-Bush. Your guidance and friendships have been integral to this project, shaping my understanding of the Enneagram and its transformative power.

My sincere appreciation also goes to my team at Psyntel: Sam Fargo, Andre Worrell, Zach Holzman, and Hayden Brown. I am so proud to be building something meaningful alongside you.

To my friends and colleagues at PEACE—founder David Kim, my fellow board members, and Sharon Kim: Thank you for your incredible work. Your commitment to promoting mental health in Asian American and Pacific Islander communities continues to inspire me.

Finally, to the team at Köehler Books, I am grateful for your belief in this book and guidance throughout the process.

REFERENCES

BOOKS

Benioff, Marc, and Carlye Adler. *Behind the Cloud: The Untold Story of How Salesforce.com Went from Idea to Billion-Dollar Company—and Revolutionized an Industry.* New York: Currency, 2009.

Benioff, Marc, and Monica Langley. *Trailblazer: The Power of Business as the Greatest Platform for Change.* New York: Currency, 2019.

Bradley, Chris, Martin Hirt, and Sven Smit. *Strategy Beyond the Hockey Stick: People, Probabilities, and Big Moves to Beat the Odds.* Hoboken, NJ: Wiley, 2018.

Broderick, Patricia C., and Pamela Blewitt. *The Life Span: Human Development for Helping Professionals.* Boston: Pearson, 2020.

Capra, Fritjof. *The Tao of Physics: An Exploration of the Parallels Between Modern Physics and Eastern Mysticism.* Boulder, CO: Shambhala Publications, 2010.

Carlsson, Sven, and Jonas Leijonhufvud. *The Spotify Play: How CEO and Founder Daniel Ek Beat Apple, Google, and Amazon in the Race for Audio Dominance.* New York: Diversion Books, 2021.

Chafkin, Max. *The Contrarian: Peter Thiel and Silicon Valley's Pursuit of Power.* New York: Penguin Press, 2021.

Chestnut, Beatrice. *The Complete Enneagram: 27 Paths to Greater Self-Knowledge.* Berkeley, CA: She Writes Press, 2013.

Christensen, Clayton M., and Michael E. Raynor. *The Innovator's Solution: Creating and Sustaining Successful Growth.* Boston: Harvard Business Review Press, 2013.

Clear, James. *Atomic Habits: An Easy & Proven Way to Build Good Habits & Break Bad Ones*. New York: Avery, 2018.

Corey, Gerald. *Theory and Practice of Counseling and Psychotherapy*. 10th ed. Boston: Cengage Learning, 2016.

Cron, Ian Morgan, and Suzanne Stabile. *The Road Back to You: An Enneagram Journey to Self-Discovery*. Downers Grove, IL: InterVarsity Press, 2016.

Doerr, John. *Measure What Matters: How Google, Bono, and the Gates Foundation Rock the World with OKRs*. New York: Portfolio, 2018.

Ferri, Richard. *All About Asset Allocation*. 2nd ed. New York: McGraw-Hill Education, 2010.

Frankl, Viktor E., William J. Winslade, and Harold S. Kushner. *Man's Search for Meaning*. Boston: Beacon Press, 2006.

Graham, Benjamin. *The Intelligent Investor: The Definitive Book on Value Investing*. Revised ed. New York: HarperBusiness, 2006.

Goldratt, Eliyahu M. *The Goal: A Process of Ongoing Improvement*. Great Barrington, MA: North River Press, 2014.

Hagstrom, Robert G. *The Warren Buffett Way*. Hoboken, NJ: Wiley, 2013.

Haskel, Jonathan, and Stian Westlake. *Capitalism without Capital: The Rise of the Intangible Economy*. Princeton, NJ: Princeton University Press, 2018.

Hawkins, Jeff, and Richard Dawkins. *A Thousand Brains: A New Theory of Intelligence*. New York: Basic Books, 2021.

Housel, Morgan. *The Psychology of Money: Timeless Lessons on Wealth, Greed, and Happiness*. Petersfield, UK: Harriman House, 2020.

Iger, Robert. *The Ride of a Lifetime: Lessons Learned from 15 Years as CEO of the Walt Disney Company*. New York: Random House, 2019.

Isaacson, Walter. *Elon Musk*. New York: Simon & Schuster, 2023.

Kiyosaki, Robert T. *Rich Dad Poor Dad: What the Rich Teach Their Kids About Money That the Poor and Middle Class Do Not!* Scottsdale, AZ: Plata Publishing, 2017.

Knight, Phil. *Shoe Dog: A Memoir by the Creator of Nike*. New York: Scribner, 2016.

Lynch, Peter. *One Up on Wall Street: How to Use What You Already Know to Make Money in the Market*. New York: Simon & Schuster, 2000.

Mayer, Christopher W. *100 Baggers: Stocks That Return 100-to-1 and How to Find Them*. Baltimore, MD: Laissez Faire Books, 2018.

Meyerson, Jeff. *Move Fast: How Facebook Builds Software*. Self-published, 2020.

Moore, Geoffrey A. *Crossing the Chasm: Marketing and Selling Disruptive Products to Mainstream Customers*. 3rd ed. New York: HarperBusiness, 2014.

Quenk, Naomi L. *Essentials of Myers-Briggs Type Indicator Assessment*. Hoboken, NJ: Wiley, 2009.

Riso, Don Richard, and Russ Hudson. *Personality Types: Using the Enneagram for Self-Discovery*. Boston: Houghton Mifflin Harcourt, 1996.

Riso, Don Richard, and Russ Hudson. *The Wisdom of the Enneagram: The Complete Guide to Psychological and Spiritual Growth for the Nine Personality Types*. New York: Bantam, 1999.

Roose, Kevin. *Futureproof: 9 Rules for Humans in the Age of Automation*. New York: Random House, 2021.

Stone, Brad. *Amazon Unbound: Jeff Bezos and the Invention of a Global Empire*. New York: Simon & Schuster, 2021.

FILMS AND TELEVISION

A Few Good Men. Directed by Rob Reiner. Columbia Pictures, 1992.

Black Swan. Directed by Darren Aronofsky. Fox Searchlight Pictures, 2010.

Bohemian Rhapsody. Directed by Bryan Singer. 20th Century Fox, 2018.

Cruella. Directed by Craig Gillespie. Walt Disney Studios, 2021.

Doctor Strange. Directed by Scott Derrickson. Marvel Studios, 2016.

Everything Everywhere All at Once. Directed by Daniel Kwan and Daniel Scheinert. A24, 2022.

Friends. Created by David Crane and Marta Kauffman. NBC, 1994–2004.

Game of Thrones. Created by David Benioff and D. B. Weiss. HBO, 2011–2019.

Hidden Figures. Directed by Theodore Melfi. 20th Century Fox, 2016.

House of Gucci. Directed by Ridley Scott. United Artists Releasing, 2021.

Inside Man. Directed by Spike Lee. Universal Pictures, 2006.

Mean Girls. Directed by Mark Waters. Paramount Pictures, 2004.

Moonstruck. Directed by Norman Jewison. Metro-Goldwyn-Mayer, 1987.

Sherlock Holmes. Directed by Guy Ritchie. Warner Bros. Pictures, 2009.

The Talented Mr. Ripley. Directed by Anthony Minghella. Paramount Pictures, 1999.

The Wizard of Oz. Directed by Victor Fleming. Metro-Goldwyn-Mayer, 1939.

Top Gun: Maverick. Directed by Joseph Kosinski. Paramount Pictures, 2022.

JOURNAL ARTICLES

Francis, Leslie J., and Andrew Village. "The Francis Psychological Type Scales (FPTS): Factor Structure, Internal Consistency Reliability, and Concurrent Validity with the MBTI." *Mental Health, Religion & Culture* 25, no. 9 (2022): 931–51. https://doi.org/10.1080/13674676.2022.2041584.

Lake, Christopher J., John Carlson, Angela Rose, and Carolyn Chlevin-Thiele. "Trust in Name Brand Assessments: The Case of the Myers-Briggs Type Indicator." *The Psychologist-Manager Journal* 22, no. 2 (2019): 91–107.

Pittenger, David J. "Cautionary Comments Regarding the Myers-Briggs Type Indicator." *Consulting Psychology Journal: Practice and Research* 57, no. 3 (2005): 210–21. https://doi.org/10.1037/1065-9293.57.3.210.

Stein, Robert, and Abigail B. Swan. "Evaluating the Validity of Myers-Briggs Type Indicator Theory: A Teaching Tool and Window into Intuitive Psychology." *Social and Personality Psychology Compass* 13, no. 8 (2019): e12434. https://doi.org/10.1111/spc3.12434.

Turner, Alice F., and Adam Elson. "Using MBTI and What It Tells Us About the Impact of Introversion on Coaching Relationships: A Provocation." *The Coaching Psychologist* 18, no. 1 (2022): 10–18.

SONGS

Swift, Taylor. "Anti-Hero." *Midnights*. Republic Records, 2022.

OTHER SOURCES

King, Martin Luther Jr. "Nobel Prize Acceptance Speech." December 10, 1964. https://www.nobelprize.org/prizes/peace/1964/king/acceptance-speech/.

Musk, Elon. Interview by Neil Strauss. *Rolling Stone*, November 15, 2017. https://www.rollingstone.com/culture/culture-features/elon-musk-the-architect-of-tomorrow-120850/.

www.ingramcontent.com/pod-product-compliance
Lightning Source LLC
LaVergne TN
LVHW041920070526
838199LV00051BA/2677